Overcoming *the* Rain

Candace Taylor

BALBOA
PRESS

A DIVISION OF HAY HOUSE

Balboa Press books may be ordered through booksellers or by contacting:

Balboa Press
A Division of Hay House
1663 Liberty Drive
Bloomington, IN 47403
www.balboapress.com
1 (877) 407-4847

Because of the dynamic nature of the Internet, any web addresses or links contained in this book may have changed since publication and may no longer be valid. The views expressed in this work are solely those of the author and do not necessarily reflect the views of the publisher, and the publisher hereby disclaims any responsibility for them.

The author of this book does not dispense medical advice or prescribe the use of any technique as a form of treatment for physical, emotional, or medical problems without the advice of a physician, either directly or indirectly. The intent of the author is only to offer information of a general nature to help you in your quest for emotional and spiritual well-being. In the event you use any of the information in this book for yourself, which is your constitutional right, the author and the publisher assume no responsibility for your actions.

Any people depicted in stock imagery provided by Thinkstock are models, and such images are being used for illustrative purposes only.
Certain stock imagery © Thinkstock.

Print information available on the last page.

ISBN: 978-1-5043-5255-0 (sc)
ISBN: 978-1-5043-5256-7 (e)

Balboa Press rev. date: 06/09/2016

I, Candace Taylor, wrote this note because this morning was the same as every other morning and I just didn't care anymore. My husband calls me stupid, my kids don't respect me and I didn't go anywhere in life. I am so tired and frustrated. I looked at that bottle of Tylenol PM and thought I might be happier dead.

Dear Charlie:

I can't take it any longer. I am unhappy with my life. I can't do anything right for you anyway. I am a complete failure, personally and professionally. Take good care of my precious kids. Tell them I love them.

Candace

I looked out the window and saw the sky becomimg cloudy and gray. The wind was bending the trees in such a way that they appeared to be alone and emotionless. Kind of like me. I feel alone even when with my family. I no longer feel any hope or any excitement. I am numb. I wonder how long Tylenol PM takes to work...or should I take something else? What shall I do? I can't stand my empty life—I'm dead anyway--and there's no way out.

I didn't know how long I sat at the table contemplating ending my life. I heard footsteps on the porch—it must be the kids coming home from school. I must have lost all track of time. Now I have to deal with them. I can't...I have to...I do love my kids very much. They deserve better than a mother like me who just works in a pizza tavern. They must be so ashamed of me. Their friends have mothers who are nurses and teachers. I slowly picked my head up from the table. "Mommy has another head-ache." "Please go do your homework in your rooms." Where did I put the Tylenol? I didn't want them to witness what I was about to do. I heard Charles say to Rose as they walked away, "Mom must be paying the bills again. She never wants to be bothered when she does that."

I heard the phone ring but I did not answer it. I heard my sister-in-law, Kayla, mumbling something into the answering machine. I didn't care what she was saying anyway...every day is the same and I won't be around much longer.

Now who was coming? I heard someone coming again. What time is it? How long have I been sitting here? My husband is home already? I will be in trouble for not having dinner cooking. I hate my life. I better get up and get moving. I must be a mess. I didn't fix my hair or put on makeup today. I didn't care what I looked like. I pushed back my disheveled hair. I should have changed my sloppy jeans and t-shirt. And I still wore my beat-up bedroom slippers. I must have looked like a train wreck. And I still didn't care. I quickly stuffed my suicide note into the back of the bill drawer.

Charlie entered the kitchen and asked, "What are you doing, Candace? You look like something the cat dragged in."

The Next Day

The next morning I took a shower and fixed myself up. I then felt a little better. As I sat with my coffee I couldn't help but think about my family. My husband is a good man. He works hard and is a good father. He does his best to provide for the family. One drawback is that he has a nasty temper. He flies off the handle so easily I am afraid to approach him at times. I never know what I am going to get. He can be nice or he can be a demon. Sometimes he gets that look in his eye when he "snaps out." He screams at me and calls me stupid. I am too timid to fight back. I just cringe and keep apologizing, even for things that aren't my fault.

My kids are good kids. They are normal, healthy and smart. Charles is a little devil at times. He is mischievous and likes to torment his sister. They both do well in school. Rose is already in 5th grade and Charles in 8th grade. Why am I so dissatisfied? I should appreciate more what I do have. I just don't feel like a success.

I think I'll see what message Kayla left on the answering machine yesterday. In her message Kayla suggested, "You and Charlie can apply for a Pell grant and go to college free on the grant." Well, Kayla ought to know-- she works at the Community College. Charlie doesn't make that much money and my job at the pizza tavern is cash under the table. What an idea! And of course, this schooling will be at the local Community College. A ray of hope to make something of myself! I will play the message for Charlie when he gets home. I hope he will be as excited as I am. I feel resurrected from the depths! I began dancing around the room. I can do this! I am going to be somebody after all! I always wanted to be a nurse. This can be my chance! I will return Kayla's call and get the ball rolling. I can't wait to fill out the application. I will explain to Charlie and cook him his favorite meal. I hope he understands how important this is to me. I hope he doesn't get mad.

I played the message for Charlie but he said, "How can you possibly attend school with a job and family." I pleaded with him that it can and will work. He isn't interested in school for himself – he is happy welding in his factory and is satisfied with his trade. However, I do not feel I am a success. I needed to be able to achieve something more with my life. School is what I need. Please, God, let Charlie let me go to school. Please let it work. When I took the kids to church I prayed extra for an answer to my request that I could make something of myself.

Charlie wouldn't go to church with us. He converted his religion to marry me. But it didn't work out for him. So now he doesn't have any church. God is important in my life. It seemed that He answered my prayers for anything important I ever prayed for. Please hear me now, Jesus.

My Request

I dreaded going to the pizza tavern tonight. Men call me "honey" and one even slapped me on the backside. Charlie would be there with a gun if he knew that. I know better than to tell him. But the tips are good and we very much need the money. I so very much want to be a nurse – a professional person who gets respect. I want to be respected. Being called "Honey" is not respect. I will do just about anything to get to go to school. Tomorrow I am going to fill out that Pell grant application and send it in no matter what Charlie says. He'll see, it will work and it will improve our lives. I have lots of stamina when I need it and I can do this!

I went to work that evening. My job at the pizza tavern brought me no respect or success. I smiled at drunks at the bar and served pizza to the clients. I also made hoagies and took people's money. Each evening was a long evening. I didn't think about the Tylenol PM. The thought of school replaced that. I could think of nothing but school. I thought how nice it would be to be a nurse instead of a waitress. I would command respect. There isn't much you can do with an Academic high school education if you don't go to college. I can't type or do book keeping. I don't have a trade. I serve pizza and beer.

My shift finally ended. I parked in front of the house. My beat-up Chrysler made it home once again. I saw a light on in the living room. Charlie was still up. If he's in a good mood it might be the time to talk to him. I entered the living room to greet him. He put his arm around me and led me upstairs to bed.

"Charlie, I want very much to go to school," I pleaded. "I will take good care of you and the kids while I am in school. I need to do this. It won't cost us any money. Please say yes. That will make me happier than anything ever could!" I turned the lamp onto low and began making love to Charlie. He responded. I didn't wait for an answer. I took that as a yes.

The Lay Off

I sat at the kitchen table to fill out the grant application. Charlie strongly refused to attend the Community College himself and no more was ever said about my attending. I carefully filled out the form and I got it ready for the mail.

I planned on dealing with Charlie again about my attending—but not until I had to.

I dreaded the next thing I had to do. That was to pay the bills. Bills, bills, and more bills--there was never enough money to cover them all. And Charles and Rose needed new sneakers for school. Some bills had to go back into the drawer. I was unable to pay them all. The kids need sneakers more. I sorted through and put aside those bills that must get paid now. Hopefully there will be enough money to cover them. We are barely scraping by. I am beginning to get the headache I usually get when I have to pay the bills. The bill drawer is so full.

I thought more about returning to school. In high school I was an academic honor student destined for college. But I fell in love so very young. Charlie was a bright vocational student training to be a welder. My girlfriend was always trying to fix me up with Charlie. I didn't particularly like him. But he was always there to give me a ride home after dark so I didn't have to walk or call Mom and Dad for a ride. And he had a hot red sports car.

Things happened. He was always on his best behavior when he was with me. Soon we were dating. The rest is history.

I really need to pay these bills and get it over with. That's enough daydreaming for me. My family will soon be home. I am feeling very much taken for granted. I can do more than cook dinner. I will show the world. But what if I fail? What if I can't make it through college? The years have gone by. And I am no longer a teenager. I am already mid-thirties. Will the work be too hard? Maybe I am not smart enough now. What if I don't get any support? Where will I get time to study? Maybe I won't show the world.

Charlie came home very quiet and glum. I wondered why he seemed different. He wouldn't talk to me. I also wondered what I did wrong now. He finally started to talk after dinner. "I was laid off from my job. There is little work in the plant. There is even talk of the plant closing permanently. "I was told I can collect but I don't know how much." I was stunned. We could not survive without Charlie's salary. We had four mouths to feed. And the kids needed shoes. And we were just getting by now. Charlie will collect unemployment for a while. I realized I needed to make more money.

A Bookstore Visit

The sun shined high in the sky – it was going to be a gem of a day. I felt optimistic about things to come. Charles and Rose were riding their bikes in the fresh air. I put on my best dress with my blue blazer on top of it. I fixed my fluffy long blonde hair and it turned out better than usual. I carefully applied makeup to look natural. I looked in the mirror and felt I was at my best.

I needed to find a better job. I planned on applying for work at the local drug store. They might want me because I can use a cash register. I also planned on applying at the large Bookstore on the other side of town. I heard that is a classy place. I can't imagine them wanting me. But you never know. I can run a cash register and be nice to people. I would need nicer clothes to work there and we can't afford that right now. I will apply anyway. You never know. I wouldn't mind that. I wonder how much they pay. If I could get a full time job with benefits for my family it would help out a lot. I only worked a couple hours 3 nights a week at the tavern. I had to get a better job.

I filled out an application at the drugstore but was told they are not hiring. Discouraged, I drove across town to "The Bookstore."

I entered the store and was taken by the clean scent of new books and potpourri. Shelves of books were everywhere. Toward the back of the store was a counter where you could buy coffee and dessert. I could almost taste the sweet smell of pastry and flavored coffee. There were tables where you could sit down and read a book or just have a drink. Yes, this was a beautiful place where I wouldn't mind spending the day. I love books. This just might work for me. I will ask at the register for an application.

I filled out the application given to me by the woman at the cash register. She didn't even smile. I wonder why she looks so glum. She works in a beautiful bookstore with books, a little coffee counter, and expensive candy bars. I wondered what her problem was.

I walked around the store just to get better acquainted with it. The plush carpeting felt rich under my feet. Customers talked freely – you didn't need to be quiet as in a library. I looked at a self-help book that seemed interesting and I read a few pages. I felt the smooth, hard cover and liked running my fingers over it. The pages were crisp and new. This would definitely beat the pizza tavern. I hoped I would get called.

I drove home and tried to come down from my experience in the bookstore. I returned to the same old life again. I was working at the tavern tonight and needed to change my clothes. The hotter I looked the hotter the tips. Out of habit I checked the answering machine for messages. The message light was on. The message was from someone from Financial Aid at the Community College stating, "Your Pell Grant has been processed and you are receiving grant money to cover tuition, fees and books for the next year. Please stop in next time you are at the school." I whooped out loud and screamed at the top of my lungs. "I am going to college." "I am going to be a nurse!" I stopped dancing for minute and became locked into thought. What do I do now? How do I get into the Nursing school? What classes do I take? How do I get into them? I will call the financial aid number on the answering machine. Maybe they will tell me how to get started. The bookstore was totally forgotten already. I want to go to school!

I tried to calm myself while I dialed the number. A woman answered, "Good afternoon, Financial Aid." "My name is Candace Taylor and I received a message that I am getting grant money for fall. I don't know what to do to get into school. Can you help me?" "Yes," said the woman. Call this number and someone there will tell you what to do to register." "Thank you."

I called again and got an appointment to see a counselor at the school. I was told this counselor will determine what classes I should take and even set me up with a schedule that will work for me. Wow! What service! I rejoiced but realized I must tell Charlie what I am doing. I will think about what to say to him very carefully. I don't want to rock the boat more than I have to.

The next thing I did was to share my good fortune with Kayla. God bless her. She gave me this opportunity. I will never forget what she did for me, no matter what. Without her I wouldn't have been going to school in the first place.

Registration

My appointment to register was here. I wore my only nice pair of pants with a lightweight short-sleeved sweater. I wanted to look nice. I hoped my counselor would be nice.

I must admit that this was the first time I actually set foot on the campus. The campus grass was very green and nicely cut. There were large bushes with colorful flowers and flower beds around buildings. The grounds were absolutely beautiful. The buildings were spaciously placed apart and each conveniently displayed a large, numeric building number. I needed to go to building 8 for registration.

"Hello, my name is Candace Taylor. I came to see a counselor to register." "Please sit down. Someone will be with you shortly."

I was called in and shook hands with Mr. Young. "I will be your counselor, Candace. It's nice to meet you." I did not hesitate to tell Mr. Young my plans. "I want to be a nurse, and I am not interested in anything else." "Let me explain to you how nursing works, he said. "You just don't just walk into the nursing program. You need to qualify and have certain courses out of the way first. I can set you up with preliminary classes. This fall you need to take your General Study Courses. Your success rate in Nursing School will be much higher." I thought to myself how disappointing this is. But I will at least have a start and will do what I have to do. Classes will start September 3rd.

Mr. Young and I picked my night classes for this fall. I am scheduled with a full-time load so I could start nursing as soon as possible. I will need to attend classes 3 nights a week. Mr. Young sensed my determination and sensed my desire to become a nurse. I must hurry now to go to something that's called an "Arena Registration."

I saw a long line going to building 11. "That must be it. I have to wait in such a long line? I must get home. I can't spend an entire day here just registering. I must go home and clean the kitchen and start dinner. Then I thought twice, "Too bad for that. I am going to do this for myself. If I want to be a nurse I must do this. I wish I had brought a book to read while I have to stand in line."

One hour later I finally made it to the front of the line. A frazzled-looking woman about 50 years old said, "May I help you?" "I came to register for class." The woman aggressively took the paper from my hand and started typing on the computer. She showed no emotion. "Miss Personality," I thought. When she finished she said, "Go to the Bookstore to get your books."

The Bookstore on campus was definitely not "The Bookstore." I laughed at myself for so loosely using the phrase "On Campus." It sounded to me like I was already a seasoned college student. There were lots of students crowding the aisles and shopping. I guess this is what I missed years ago. Now I am an adult and I realized that I missed all that. A clerk helped me find my books and I was headed home. I felt as though I missed part of my life that I was supposed to experience. But I had my books and looked forward to starting my classes. I, Candace Taylor, a college student!

My Worries

I had enough excitement for one day. I needed to be home and spend some time with my family. After dinner I invited everybody to a game of softball in the backyard. Charles and Rose are great kids. I love them dearly. Charlie has been helpful around the house while he is off from work and I needed some time with him too.

Charlie was in the kitchen. I started to tell him about my day but he cut me off. "I don't see this working," he said. "You belong here at home. You are a wife and mother."

I just had so much going on. I had to worry about my upcoming interview with the dean. I needed a new outfit for this but we couldn't afford it. I had to go to work that same evening. God knows we need the money. What will I do if Charlie doesn't cooperate with school? I am registered and already have my books. I must be a model wife and mother so I can go to school too.

The Bookstore Interview

Work was pretty much routine. I got a good night's sleep and made breakfast for Charlie and the kids. Right after 9 o'clock the phone rang. Hello, this is Cindy calling from "The Bookstore." "Miss Brook would like to interview you at 2 o'clock today. You applied for a position as a clerk."

I felt very grateful. What will I wear? I need to look good. I must go shopping. I will go to Macy's and get something very professional. I don't have the money but we do have a credit card. I promised Charlie I wouldn't put anything new on the card. But this is special. I must look my best.

I tried on many outfits at the mall. I decided to buy one of the skirt suits. I thought it would be perfect. The suit I chose was a deep burgundy with a very light black stripe. It had the longer jacket that looked so classy. I completed the outfit with low black pumps. I hope Charlie approves. I hoped that Miss Brook will approve.

I drove to "The Bookstore." My nerves were beginning to get the best of me. I needed this job and the paycheck that went with it. I parked the car, took a deep breath, and went in. My senses were again taken by the scent and atmosphere of the place. The same glum looking person I had seen at the cash register greeted me and asked, "Are you here for an interview?" I answered "yes" and remembered she had given me the application. "My name is Cindy." I noticed a door to the back of the store. That must be the manager's office. I would soon find out. I wished my heart would stop thumping. I wondered if anyone else could hear it. What if I fell over my heels?

I hoped I wouldn't make a fool out of myself. I needed this job. I noticed it was already 2:05. The phone rang by the cash register. "I will take you in to see Miss Brook."

Miss Brook was standing behind her desk. I estimated her to be about 5'7" and about 180 pounds. She was wearing a simple print dress. Her reddish-blond hair was cut short but left a little longer in the back. Her skin was tanned and somewhat wrinkled. She appeared to be about 55 years old. She smiled and said "You must be Candace." "I'm Angel Brook, have a seat." She extended her hand to shake hands. My heart was still pounding and my hands were now clammy.

What brought you to "The Bookstore?" asked Angel. "I need a job." I nervously stammered. Angel smiled rather sweetly and said, "You must be applying for my job all dressed up like that." I just cringed at the words. "I'm just kidding," said Angel. If you get hired you won't need to dress like that. "What experience do you have? " "I can run a cash register and I like books." "That's better," said Angel. "I see from your application you work at a pizza tavern. However, this is a class place. You must act professional, look good, and be able to be nice to the customers." I managed a smile and said "I am used to doing that. I would love to work for you, Miss Brook." "Call me Angel. I will review your application and let you know my decision."

I thought about Charlie and the kids. My family needs me to get this job. I wonder what kind of impression I made. At least I didn't fall over my shoes. In the same breath I need to worry about school clothes for Charles and Rose. I have to get the kids more school clothes. And it looks like I need to take the credit card out again. If I get the job in "The Bookstore" I will need suitable clothes also.

The next day was Saturday. Charlie and I took the kids for school clothes and a cheap fast food supper. Then I took the kids to church. I was alone with the kids in church and without Charlie as usual. I can't even talk to him about God. He gets loud and mean and just puts me down. He never wants to talk about religion. I know he is sorry he changed his religion for me. He only talks about everyday things with me. He doesn't even share his dreams if he has any. Charlie is a very private man. He doesn't always let me in.

At home Charlie said, "There is a message on the answering machine for you. "You know I can't hear well." I played the message —"This message is for Candace. This is 'The Bookstore. "When you receive this message please return the call."

I nervously called "The Bookstore" stating my name as Candace Taylor. I was put on hold. Angel came on the phone. "Candace? I hope you are ready to come and work with us. I am offering you a job as Bookstore Clerk. I couldn't see bringing you in again to tell you this. Do you still want a job?" I practically screamed out "yes!" "Good," said Angel. You start Wednesday, September 3rd. 8:00 – 4:00. By the way, come dressed to work. No jeans and no dresses. And especially don't wear a suit." My heart dropped. That was the same day I started school.

Back to Reality

I called Kayla for advice as to how I would be able to do all this. She offered to help Charlie with the kids at night if he needed to go somewhere. And, kind person that she always was, she told me she is getting rid of some very nice clothes and that I was welcome to them. "Thank you, Kayla. I didn't know what I would do for some new clothes." Kayla was always there when I needed her.

Summer turned out to be hectic with interviews and worrying and planning my new life style. I have been neglecting Charlie to a degree. He has his hobbies and is great with the housework and the kids. Maybe when I am a success I will feel better about everything. Charlie told me he has a job interview tomorrow as a security guard. I hope that works out for him. It may be better for him than being a factory worker and it is certainly better than unemployment.

I sat at the same kitchen table that only a few weeks ago I wanted my life to end. The sun shone through the window making the kitchen really look shabby. I looked at the small kitchen closet that had to hold everything from food to winter coats. It was always a mess because there just wasn't enough room within. We both had to do better. I shouldn't have settled for a life like this. I was intended for better things. I really messed up. But now I am pointed in the right direction.

I know it isn't going to be easy. Charlie is going to get the brunt of this. After he works all day he has to take care of the kids three nights a week. He will have to make dinner. They will be just starting back to school. And their Mom won't be available. They still need me. What if they need help with their homework? My classes are all set to go. If I don't do this now I probably never will. Maybe I wouldn't get the Financial Aid if I waited a few years. Charlie would never let me spend the money to pay for school for myself. What if my kids get messed up because I'm not here? Maybe I could come home between my new job and class and throw together a dinner. Then I will be home by 9:30. That's not too late. Charlie will still be up and I will see him. If need be, I can help the kids with homework in the morning. I will give everyone breakfast before we start our days. I must get very efficient and organized. We need the money and I desperately want the schooling. Why do things have to happen all at once? I can't give up a decent job offer. We very much need the money and benefits. Please, God, give me strength.

Getting Organized

Charlie, Charles and Rose came home from Kayla's house. The kids were full of excitement. Kayla bought them some extra school clothes and new book bags. Charlie didn't seem to enjoy excitement, as he always loudly and abruptly quieted it when the kids got excited. I never understood why he did this. Kids should get excited. It's their feelings coming out.

I did understand he was nervous about his job interview in the morning. I had hoped he would find work that would prove to be exciting for him. I told him he had to get a dayshift job because of my going to school. I just got a scowl. A little role reversal seems to be present and Charlie is used to being the one who provides the most for the family. I know he secretly resents my chance at success. I am supposed to be the "little woman."

Morning came and Charlie went to his interview. I wished him luck and told him I was proud of him. He went off feeling good about himself.

I spent my day trying on the clothes Kayla had given me. They were stylish and looked good. Since I had already given my notice at the pizza tavern I was free this evening. My job at "The Bookstore" and school started tomorrow. The kids were to go back to school after Labor Day. I decided what I would wear to the first day of work and started cleaning. Then I thought about how I would get the cleaning done while working and going to school. I will be so busy.

Charlie came home with a smile and said, "I was offered the security job at the mall. It is 7:00 a.m. to 3:00 p.m. What do you think? I smiled back and said, "That will be perfect. I can put the kids out and you can be home when they get home."

"I hope you are going to accept the job." I rejoiced in the fact that Charlie will be working and our lives will start to fall into place. The kids were a big worry. But now that seems it will work out. I explained to Charles and Rose that someone will be home for them both before and after school. Mom and Dad will be starting new jobs and I will be going to school three nights a week. I hoped to eventually become an RN. In the meantime I will be working in a very nice Bookstore and you can tell that to your friends. Mommy will no longer be working in the pizza tavern. We will have more money. Dad will be making more money also, so things won't be so tight. School starts in a few days, so enjoy the rest of your summer. I felt positive.

My First Day at The Bookstore

The day quickly arrived. My first day to work at The Bookstore was here. My very first day of college was here. School was on the back burner for now as I must concentrate on getting ready for work. Candace Taylor was finally working in a classy place. I needed to look classy also. I chose one of the nice outfits Kayla gave me. I chose simple black pants and a bright blue wrap shirt. I put it on and had to admit—it looked good. Should I wear my hair in a ponytail or wear it down? I decided to wear it down. I was ready. I was ready to work in a classy place.

I arrived at the Bookstore 15 minutes early to make a good first impression. I "reported for duty" butterflies and all. Cindy, the secretary was already in the store and opened the door for me. "Welcome. Kevin will be here any minute. He will show you the important things like where the coffee pot is kept." We both smiled. But where was my boss? As though Cindy read my mind, she said "Angel doesn't get here this early. You have a lot to learn. We'll leave it at that." Kevin walked in and escorted me to the back room where much of the preliminary work was done. The packing, unpacking, receiving, returning, pricing and ordering would eventually become part of my job. It sounded like fun. He also told me that Angel did most of the ordering but Kevin was allowed to "recommend" supplies such as pens and notebook paper.

Cindy took her place at her desk and immediately started looking through a fat folder. It was full of bills. "I pay bills every Monday morning."

Kevin and I went into the store. Customers would soon be coming. The store looked so bright and pretty. I imagined only affluent people would shop here. We walked all around the store to familiarize me with the merchandise. There were lots of books, of course. There were magazines and art supplies, and cards and backpacks. There were knick knacks and expensive chocolates. I smelled the coffee brewing in the little café. I thought the store was just great. Then Kevin said "Angel wanted you to learn the cash register today. We all work the cash register. So you need to learn it also."

I happily accepted the cash register training. I learned quickly because the machine was similar to the one I used at the pizza tavern. Thoughts of the tavern sent chills down my spine. I am done with that. I now work in a class place. I feel so happy to be here. I rang up my first customer. It was a book about Africa. I smiled at her and she smiled back. I can do this. This is good.

When the customer left the store I thought about Angel. I really only met her the day she hired me. Thinking back to that day, she may be one of those people where you never know what you're going to get. She was almost too sweet until she told me about my suit. I'm sure time will tell.

Angel rolled in about 9:30 looking like a frenzied cat. She immediately went to her office and didn't come out for at least one half hour. She then approached me at the cash register. She was "too" nice. "I'm so glad to see you here, Candace. How is it going? Did Kevin show you the store? Do you like it?" Before I had a chance to answer she was already walking away. "For this week just wait on customers and operate the cash register. If anyone wants something wrapped as a gift, we do gift wrap. That is your job also." Whew! What a whirlwind! Kevin came out and gave me a tip to tidy up the candy and straighten the displays whenever Angel is around. She believes in keeping busy. Lunch time came and with the bookstore located in a big shopping center I could window shop on my lunch hour. There was a cozy restaurant a few doors down but I couldn't afford to eat there as a habit. I would eat my bag lunch in my car. This could work out great at Christmas. Oh, I start school tonight! Here I am in dreamland. I still wanted to be a nurse. As nice as The Bookstore is, I don't want to be a sales clerk for the rest of my life. I will briefly see my family before I have to leave for school. It's lucky I prepared a tuna noodle casserole for dinner tonight. I hope he doesn't get mad. I told him that school starts tonight.

Back at the bookstore business was slow. I observed Angel through the curtains on her office window. She was animatedly talking on the phone. I tried not to make any judgments. This was my first day and I needed the job. My shift came to a close. I was snootily relieved by the part time clerk coming on duty. She informed me that she applied for my job but didn't get it. I clumsily apologized and quickly left the store. I counted my blessings that I didn't have to work with her.

Back home I was bursting to tell my family about my first day. The kids were noisy and Charlie was quiet. I put the hot tuna noodle casserole onto the table and I served everyone. The kids started eating. Charlie took one forkful, left the table carrying his plate and scraped the food into the garbage. He put his plate in the sink and walked away without a word. I held back the tears.

College Begins

I arrived on campus still hurting from Charlie's insult. Charles and Rose were starting their homework as I left. I knew Charlie would oversee them adequately. It is too bad I have a bad start to my first class since high school.

I knew where building four was located. I slowly approached the building with anticipation. I needed to forget what happened at home and to concentrate on what was happening now. I need to be here both body and mind. I easily found Room 419. Six students were already seated at the back of the room. Most noticeable to me were two adult students in the mix, one male and one female. I felt better knowing I wouldn't be sitting with all "kids." My first inclination was to join people in the back row. From somewhere, I got the courage to sit in the first row. I heard from somewhere that the best learning occurs in front of the class. I could certainly use all the help I could get.

Students entered one at a time, eventually filling up the class. On my schedule, my professor was posted as Dr. David Moore. The palms of my hand were getting clammy with perspiration. If only I had more support. I put that out of my mind.

Professor Moore entered the room. He was about 5'6" in height and slightly stocky. He wore khakis with a coordinating plaid dress shirt. He wore brown dock sider loafers. Very appropriate, I thought. He appeared to be younger than me, late 20's or so. Sitting in front I got a better look at his face. His reddish brown hair was balding on top. He was clean shaven and wore glasses. He had nice even facial features, no feature too extreme. No feature too anything. He appeared to be pleasant and comfortable in his own skin. My first impression was a positive one.

The professor wrote his name on the blackboard. Dr. David Moore, English 102, Literature. He spoke. I noted he spoke with a nice British accent. "Good evening, students. Welcome to Introduction to Literature." My name is Dr. David Moore and I allow my evening students to call me 'David.' I think that puts us all on the same page for learning." We will learn and have fun too. I am going to pass out my syllabus." The professor smiled. He had a nice smile too. Class got underway. David said, "We will study poetry, short stories and drama, with poetry being first. Also, each of you will have to write a research paper. We will go over research paper how-to each week. The due date is the end of the semester.

David read us a poem from our Literature book. I couldn't remember the title, but when he read poetry he made it sound like a song. I was transfixed at the smooth words that came out of his mouth.

Class ended with an assignment to read several selected poems and to explicate each one as what it means to each of us. There would be a quiz next week on one of the assigned poems. We could expect a quiz each week on something.

I left class so inspired I wanted to start the homework immediately. However, that turned out to be impossible. I resolved to go home and be extra nice to Charlie. I was sure that this wasn't easy for him. I need to make school work out for both of us. He is my husband. And I am Charlie's wife. I can't leave him in the dust.

Aftermath of the First Class

I arrived home and parked in my spot in front of the house. I was in a good mood, still thinking about the sound of the words coming from David's mouth. It was only 9:00, as class left out a little early. I didn't hear any sounds of activity in the house. I walked up the steps and found Charles and Rose already sleeping. Charlie, too was already in bed but still awake. I greeted him, "Hello. I see you have everything under complete control. I am so happy you did this." Charlie stared at me with cold eyes. "Don't bother me." Oh, no, My heart sank. We were destined to have one of those arguments again. "Don't be mad at me Charlie, you were wonderful to take care of the kids and let me go to school." "Don't bother me," he repeated.

I left our bedroom. Usually we have a big blow-out before the silence starts. Charlie yells and throws in everything I ever did wrong to him. He calls me names, especially "stupid." Then we don't talk for several days. This time it went right to silence without the blowout. I know school is the problem. It has to be. I don't think he would get that mad over tuna casserole.

I need to go to school in two nights too. This problem needs to be resolved. The trouble is that we never resolve anything. We fight, go into silence for a few days then gradually go back to "normal." Nothing ever gets resolved.

I showered and put on a sexy nightgown. I got into bed and put my arm around Charlie. He quickly pushed me away without a word. I rolled over and tried to get some sleep.

My Inventory Project

What should I do? Charlie still wasn't talking when we got up for work. I think I'll call Kayla tonight. She always knew what to do. In the meantime I still had to go to work. Thank God I didn't have class tonight, but I will have it the next night. I planned on acting like nothing is wrong. That sometimes works.

I looked forward to going to work. I knew I had a lot to learn and was more than willing to learn it. I arrived at the store and as usual Angel wasn't in yet. Kevin informed me that Angel said I would be working on the inventory. Although I did need to learn "the back room" I also needed to learn inventory. I never worked on inventory before. Kevin told me that Angel would show me. He didn't know everything about it but said all the invoices for the entire year were saved up and put in order by date, oldest invoices on top. Then you needed to determine what was still in the store and what was sold out. Kevin said he was clueless as to how this was done. The computer listing needed to reflect only what was in the store. And the entire store got lined up according to the listing. That sounded like an awfully big job to me.

I realized Cindy was the woman at the cash register who looked so miserable the day I was hired. She seemed nice. I will have to wait and see. And I will also have to wait and see what kind of thing could make her so glum.

I was stationed at the cash register until Angel came in. I didn't mind that job at all. I could still be working at the pizza tavern.

Angel walked in and said hello. She immediately went into her office for a few minutes then sent Kevin to get me. I entered her office and was directed to shut the door. She spoke, "Candace, I have chosen you to take charge of the inventory for this year. You struck me as very bright and I think you can do it. It is a job that brings with it much responsibility but much satisfaction. I will trust you as the kind of person who can work independently. I will always be here to answer any questions or help with any snags you run into. Do you feel up to the job?"

I was astounded. Who would have thought to give me a responsible job like that? "I will do my best," I said to Angel. I hoped I could do the job I promised I could.

I decided to delve right in and look at all the invoices first. Kevin had already said that the oldest ones may be already sold out. I decided to check by invoice and if there was any merchandise in the store I would then check the computer listing to see if it was printed. If not, I would start a list of merchandise to be added. If the price changed, I would change the price on the listing then later change the price in the computer. I would have to receive training for the computer work. But I wouldn't worry about that now. My work just started. I have come a long way from the pizza tavern in a very short time.

The first invoice was for 5 different titles of books. I searched the store for the books and realized I didn't know how to find them. I asked Kevin for help. He said to look for the book by subject. Not always an easy task. I found four of the five books and hoped the book I couldn't find was sold. I planned on double-checking everything after I was done. Angel was so right about it being a big job. It is a large, tedious job. And everything must line up exactly right in the store when it is time to count everything. Although I was a little disillusioned about the kind of work, it was a chance to prove myself. I would prove that I am smart and can do things on my own. I, Candace Taylor was in charge of the inventory of this incredible Bookstore.

Inventory Continues

Back at home things got better with Charlie. His anger and sarcasm blew over and things were kind of back to normal. We even had plans to go for pizza on Friday night with the kids. We also had plans to attend church as a family on Sunday. Charlie normally did not attend church with us, so this was special. I tried to give the kids a religious background that they could have for life. I wanted them to have something.

School was fair in my estimation. I was so determined to get an A in English. I so very much admired David and his knowledge that I very much wanted to impress him. Unfortunately, I only came up with a "B" in the poetry test and was bitterly disappointed. We already started short stories. We were assigned to read "Guests of the Nation" by Frank O'Connor and "A Rose for Emily" by William Faulkner. After that we would study some poetry and some short stories by Edgar Allan Poe. I looked forward to that. I liked Poe in high school.

I was still waiting to hear about starting nursing school next semester. My other classes were easy for me, it was just that English!

In my heart I knew I had to continue to be "Super wife" and "Supermom" for all this to continue. At times I felt tired but I chose to ignore it. Perseverance had to pay off. I had to keep going. There are things I want to do in life, places to be. I don't want to be a slave to a house. Especially to my house. Someday we would have a better house. For that to happen I had to keep going. I kept plenty of coffee on hand.

Another work/school week arrived. With everyone already gone I got dressed for work. Upon arrival I started right in on the inventory. I decided to organize one section at a time starting with easier sections first to get the practice. Kevin and I were working together. I gave him an organized listing and he would physically put everything into place in the store. He was so nice to work with.

It was almost lunch time. I was still thinking about the "B" I got in the poetry test. B's do not bring A's. I went into the book area of the store and who did I find but the Professor David himself in the store. I said hello and he greeted me by name right away. We both smiled. David told me he frequents The Bookstore quite often because he was an avid reader and keeps a large library at home. For a book he wants to keep in his library he buys the hard cover edition when available. We talked congenially about books for a few minutes. I mentioned I was disappointed with my "B" grade and wished I could do better. David smiled. There is a science in getting better grades. I would be happy to show you how you can do this. Do you get a break or lunch hour from work? I happily told him my lunch hour is from 12:00 to 1:00 most days. David said "I am available on Monday, Wednesday and Friday at that time because I have a break from classes. Would any of those days work for you? I can give you a few pointers that will help you."

I was ecstatic. David himself would help me to get better grades. I quickly said, "Any of those days would be good." David suggested, "Meet me at the restaurant in the mall strip on Wednesday at 12:00. We can grab a sandwich and I will give you some tips on study habits." I quickly accepted.

The rest of the day I was floating on air. My inventory work went oh so smoothly. I looked forward to going home and making a nice dinner for my family. Charlie and I were getting along better and that seemed smooth also. I also looked forward to my meeting with David.

The Restaurant

I arrived at the Brook Briar Restaurant. It was the first time I ever actually went in. There was a cash register on a counter near the entrance. To the left was a sign that said "Please wait for hostess to seat you." I waited by the entrance and told the hostess I was waiting for someone. "Would you like to wait at your table or take a seat in the corner right here?" I decided to take a seat in the corner. If he didn't show up I wouldn't feel as foolish.

David did show up five minutes later. He signaled me over and ordered a quiet table for two. I noticed he was a take charge person, very sure of himself. We were seated in a cozy booth in the back, away from the other diners. He was carrying a zippered binder whose contents included a legal pad, pens, and some papers in the three-hole binder section. I felt poorly prepared as I didn't bring anything. David seemed to know and gave me the legal pad and a pen. He smiled. "I brought these for you."

I ordered a turkey wrap and David ordered a turkey sandwich. Our tastes must be similar, at least as far as food goes. David started to talk. "One of the most important things you can do to learn material is to recopy your notes. When I was in school I learned to take notes on a legal pad and to later recopy them into a notebook. The repetition will help you to remember and you can research any details you missed in class. In your mind re-experience my class as you recopy the notes. This would be like remembering the nice lunch we just had. You can enjoy the taste again in your mind. Just as your taste moves to finer food so would your mind be moved to higher education. Put all the information together and you have a something you can really study from. Also, pace your studying. Study new material every night. Do not wait until two days before the test. Know your material so well the day before the test that you won't even be studying the night before. This cuts down on stress so you don't panic when handed the exam. You will be confident you know your stuff. Also, study pictures and charts. They stick in your mind better than words in a paragraph. Your mind can reproduce the picture or chart from the paper. Don't be afraid to use this."

Our food came. We continued to discuss study habits over lunch. It was a very pleasant lunch. As we parted we both stated we would enjoy lunch again. David walked me back to the Bookstore with a "See you in class!"

I felt that was so nice of David to do that. I really liked him. I liked his British accent. I liked how smooth he was. I liked his intellect. I wanted to see him again. He brought an indescribable something out in me that I hadn't felt before. I felt so intrigued by him. There existed a definite chemistry.

His advice turned out to be invaluable. One thing worried me: How can I study every night when I either have class or need to spend time with the family? It's was time to think about family. Somehow I vowed to do this. It was time to change hats again.

Old Friend/New Friend

The most sensitive man I'd ever met proved to be quite insensitive as far as my feelings were concerned. Either that or he just never realized how important he had become to me. Or else he doesn't know himself as well as he claims to.

David still continues to meet me at the restaurant for lunch in the Bookstore mall. We have come to know each other personally very well. He always reflects how important his wife and young daughter were to him. I know this as we have frequently talked about his family and how intertwined they all were with his wife's family. His own family was very small and his wife's family became his family.

Lately he has been glowingly talking about the new English professor at school and about how impressed he is with her. Ironically, her name is Candace. He describes her as young, beautiful, blonde, blue-eyed, technology oriented and never been married. He describes her personality as being much like his own. She likes to kid and joke around. She too is talkative as he is. David told me about how they frequently they kicked each other under the table during a faculty meeting. My silent thought was that they must have been sitting pretty close at the table to have that happen. Why did he share this with me? Was that relative to our friendship? I doubt he would ever make a serious move on a woman given his family situation. He has too much to lose. Her name continues to come up in our conversation. David and I have been good friends, but that's all. Our relationship has always been completely platonic. I understand my fond feelings about him. He helped me to find myself. He gave me wings so I could fly. I'll always be grateful for that. As far as his feelings go, I guessed he liked me. Or he wouldn't meet me for lunch and talk to me about philosophy, politics, religion or his work. He spent much of his own time teaching me about good study habits and actually helped me raise my letter grade. How could I not care about him? What did he get out of that? Being a teacher he probably would have done that for anyone. So I'm probably not even special to him as far as that goes. I feel like the old shoe in the corner. He has a bright, shiny new object to focus his attention on now. I keep hearing "Candace" but the name Candace is not me. It is "the other Candace." I guess I feel slighted. I never heard him say he was ever impressed with me.

I allowed him to become too important to me. That was my first mistake. I very much enjoyed his attention. I let my guard down and my feelings open. He always seemed to understand women better than most men do. I told him "secrets" about myself I never told to anyone else. I could talk to him better than any man I ever became acquainted with. I guess that's what happens. When you leave yourself open you risk being hurt. Now I need to build a little wall to protect myself. I need to protect myself from wincing whenever he talks about the shiny new object, Candace. I will smile while I'm hurting in knowing I do not mean to him what he does to me. As a true friend I will support him in wherever his desires take him. Friendships can be difficult. I know I am a very sensitive woman and that may be contributing to my hurt feelings. Is that what made it so difficult? Is the problem my own insecurity? Or are all men alike?

Knowing him has caused me to grow. I would never have wanted to miss the experience of getting to know him. I am much better for it. I acknowledge that he can surely have as many friends as he wishes, both male and female. I guess my hurt feelings stem from no longer feeling special or being as important in his life. I wonder if at one time I was ever the bright, shiny object. That seems doubtful.

But maybe that is good. Bright, shiny objects lose their luster and get replaced periodically when they lose their newness and shininess. I feel as though I am being replaced now. New relationships are always forming and old relationships may get boring. Maybe I have become boring. We talked so much maybe there is nothing exciting left to talk about. I have never been a joke around, kid around type of personality. I can't change myself. I know those people are more fun. I am a serious kind of personality. I am a good listener, not a talker. I know talkers are more fun. I am kind of quiet. In any case, I am not changing myself and I cannot change him. I will just have to see what develops. There is nothing else I can do.

Before the Rain

Back at work, I tried to finish setting up the store for the inventory. Kevin and I agreed to complete setting up the writing instruments and then proceed to the notebooks. Office supplies would be the last section to be written up. I would then be ready to enter everything remaining into the computer, a job I didn't mind at all. That part was fun. I was proud of my work and enjoyed working independently. I knew I did a good job.

Lunch time came. I needed to do a little shopping but wished I were meeting David instead. I missed him and noticed that our meetings were getting further apart.

Tonight at home, our son was having dinner at a friend's house then going shopping with the family. Charlie, Rose, and I would be home together. It was a rare evening that I didn't have school. Charlie and I needed to spend more time together. Sometimes we seemed like strangers. I was often afraid of ticking him off and of him yelling at me or calling me stupid. Hopefully tonight could be some time for renewal.

I planned popcorn and a movie after dinner. As much as I needed the quiet evening, I worried about being behind on the research paper. Edgar Allan Poe's short story, "The Fall of the House of Usher" was embedded in my mind. There were only so many hours in the day and I had so much to do. I started making coffee at night so I could stay awake after everyone went to bed. It was then I worked on my assignments. Charlie didn't say much about my schedule but now and then he would make a snide remark about "burning the candle at both ends." We have been drifting apart because our interests are so different and we haven't had much time together.

The three of us started watching the movie. The phone rang. "Is this Mrs. Taylor?" "Yes," I answered. "Do you have a son named Charles?" My heart dropped. "This is Mr. Brown, Manager of the department store. Your son is implicated in a shoplifting incident. You need to come get him." My hands were shaking. Charlie would be furious but I had to tell him.

Charlie, Rose and I drove to the department store with heavy hearts. Charlie loudly put down Charles throughout the ride. I wouldn't dare defend him or I would have Charlie's wrath for days. And besides, we still didn't know what happened.

We entered the store and asked to see the store manager. We were escorted to a back room. There was Charles with his three cronies. The young man with them introduced himself as Mr. Brown. He began speaking. It seemed three boys convinced "John" to steal a music CD and hide it in his coat. They told him they would beat him up if he didn't do it. All of them are as guilty as John. Each of the boys showed remorse and assured Mr. Brown that it wouldn't happen again.

Fortunately for all involved, Mr. Brown was a young, empathetic manager who talked to the boys as if they were his own. He stated he didn't want to ruin the record of any 13 year old if this could be resolved without prosecution. He also stated he will not prosecute THIS TIME but if it happens again he will.

Charlie and I profoundly thanked Mr. Brown and assured him that his kindness would not be forgotten. The ride home was tortuous to say the least. I could tell that Charles was truly sorry. Charlie's stony silence was worse than any yelling he could have done.

At home we prepared for bed and retired early. There would be no research paper tonight.

I woke up in beads of sweat in the middle of the night. I got a glass of water. My nerves were shot. I worried about the inventory. It needed to be completed within two days. After that everything in the store needed to be counted within three days. Then the auditors came to check the store and check counts. I absolutely needed to complete the Research Paper. Not only did I need a good grade but DAVID would be reading it. It needed to be outstanding. I was wide awake...I opened "An Introduction to Literature 8ed." As I tried to read, I found my concentration to be poor. I was just wasting my time. I went back to bed and tried to get some sleep. I lay there awake for some time before dozing off. My alarm clock too soon went off.

At work, Angel was following me around. "Is it done yet? How does it look? Counting starts in two days. Is everything in the computer?" "Where was she the last two months?" I wondered. Thus far she had trusted my progress reports but now she was getting antsy. She even followed me into the ladies room calling, "Candace, are you in there?"

Trouble seems to find me. At home Rose brought home a failed math test. "What happened?" I asked her. "I just don't understand subtraction, Mom." "We will work on this." I had to run out to school myself in half an hour. Charlie exploded. "If you paid more attention to those kids instead of having your nose in the book all the time, this would not have happened. It was your fault."

As if I didn't already feel guilty enough. I try hard to stay out of trouble with Charlie but I always fail. I know he wants the little wife who stays home and is content to cook and clean. He didn't want me to grow intellectually. But I did. And I like it. I need more than to be a housewife.

I went to school with a resolve to help Rose tomorrow and to work on the Research Paper after class. I made a pot of strong coffee and burned the midnight oil. I actually accomplished quite a bit of work and went to bed at two a.m. But it still wasn't perfect enough.

Inventory Stress

I excused myself to use the ladies room at work. While still inside the stall, Angel whined out, "Candace, are you in here?" "Yes," I said. What are you working on?" I would have liked to say "I am going to the bathroom now." But I didn't. "I will be right out." I couldn't believe Angel would bother me in the bathroom. Angel said, "Work on the cards today." I agreed even though I wasn't yet ready to work on the cards. I wondered why Angel started bothering me recently. I didn't need the aggravation. I had plenty of that at home.

I found lining up the cards to be a great deal of work. There were some very old cards that were priced differently from the newer cards. Many of the old cards weren't even on her listing. They were a mess to straighten out. I still took great pride in my work and wanted everything to be perfect.

A handsome male sales rep came into the store and Angel ran out to greet him. She extended her hand with a big smile and a sugary "Hello." "It's so nice to have you in our store. Won't you come into my office," Candace was working just outside Angel's office and could hear every word. Angel applied some of the oldest tricks known to women to wrap a man around her little finger. She gave the salesman her full attention, hanging on his every word. She looked up at him with flirtatious eyes and invited him to guide her with merchandise choices for the store. She led him on by asking him lots of questions and appealing to his "superior intellect." She pushed her chair up close to his and kept touching his arm for emphasis. That was the first time Candace ever saw her in action like that. "What a fake!" Candace thought. It disturbed her to think intelligent men fell for that routine. That was as old as the hills

I was satisfied that inventory was ready. Of course, I assumed I would oversee the process as I had for the previous two months. Kevin and I did an exceptional job. I'm proud of my work. I can do things. I am not stupid.

The Choke Cherries

Charles called to ask if he could go to Jeff's house after school. "No problem, Charles. Be good and I'll see you tonight." I planned an easy pasta dish for dinner so I would have plenty of time to help Rose with math and work on my paper.

Charles came home with his three friends about 7:00. He looked funny. "Charles, do you feel OK?" I asked. "I feel like I'm going to puke." He then promptly vomited on the floor. "Let me take your temperature." His friend, Jeff spoke up. He was eating choke cherries off my Dad's bush. We all were. Charles could barely stand. I quickly called the Poison Control Center for instructions. It seemed like an eternity before I got to talk to someone. "I don't have choke cherries listed anywhere. Do you have the name of the bush?" "No." Charles vomited again. "Take him to the nearest ER."

Charlie walked in the door. "We need to rush Charles to the ER. He was poisoned by eating choke cherries." The four of us rushed to the car. We practically flew to the ER. After a short wait and much anxiety we were admitted to the exam room. Charles vomited. The nurse motioned Charles to get up on the exam table. When the doctor entered the room, Charlie, Rose, and I were asked to leave.

After twenty minutes of being on pins and needles, the doctor beckoned us to come back in. Charles was lying on a bed. "Your son is intoxicated," the doctor said. "If he doesn't vomit more, I will have to pump his stomach. Charles then vomited a large amount. The doctor then said, "He seems to be safe now. It's lucky for him he is so young. It's lucky for you I think you had nothing to do with this incident. Therefore, I am not going to report this even though I could. The doctor was angry. Get him out of here. My advice to you is to keep better track of your son. Amen.

Inventory Day

I went to work the next day. Inventory day was here and I was very proud of my work. The store was lined up and the listing was perfect. All I had to do was look at the list and every item was in its place. Each item now had to be counted and the total count written next to each item. I planned on entering the count for each item into the computer. Extra help came in to count sections. They were all lined up against the wall, reminding me of a firing squad.

Angel took the list from me and told me to go out into the store and get ready to count. I was horrified. It was my inventory. Angel started passing out sections of the inventory to be counted by the extra help. She walked around giving orders for each section and did not even acknowledge my hard work. "You are counting office products and pencils," she said.

One of the extra people entered the counts into the computer. Angel took all the credit. I was devastated. I went home and cried my eyes out.

I did go to work the next day. The auditors came and counted a few items. Everything was perfect. Angel beamed. She gave orders to put back everything where it was before. I didn't feel like I was in my own body. I didn't want to be at work. I didn't want to be anywhere. I didn't know what I wanted. I just couldn't find peace. The store reopened. Angel told me to sit at the cash register. I remembered the glum look on Cindy's face when I came for the job interview. I certainly found out. I couldn't even imagine what I looked like.

The part timer finally came in and relieved me. I heard a song playing on the radio. "That song is on again. What is it Kevin? It was "'Venus' by Bananarama." This station plays it often."

I felt I was supposed to hear that song for a reason. I usually listen to the music and don't pay much attention to the lyrics. But this time I listened closely:

> Yeah, baby she's got it
> She's got it
> I'm your Venus, I'm your fire
> At your desire

I had a difficult time trying to concentrate. Kevin told me I was laughing to myself at the cash register. I was so ashamed at what happened with the inventory. I somehow finished out the workday and went home. I didn't want to be bothered with anybody. I just wanted everybody to leave me alone—alone in my own little world. But of course, that was impossible.

Later at Home

I rushed home to throw together some kind of dinner because it was class night. I talked to Charles and Rose about school while I cooked. I knew I wasn't spending enough time with them and felt guilty. I must start working on the research paper intensively. David would go over some requirements tonight. I planned to stay up late and work on the paper while class was fresh in my mind. I must read so I can choose that perfect and elusive thesis I just couldn't come up with.

Class proved to be interesting. We were studying short stories. These pieces of literature proved to be as thought provoking as the poems had been. I still had a hard time understanding symbolism and stressed because of it. I only scored a "B" on the last test. I needed to get an "A". I must do better. My research paper must be excellent. I could not settle for less.

After class I said good night to the family and set all the library books on the kitchen table. I must find a thesis tonight. I don't care if I have to stay up half the night. Since the class was studying short stories I read "The Cask of Amontillado," and "The Fall of the House of Usher. I was intrigued by the house of Usher. I had books with interpretations concerning this short story. "This is it!" I said out loud. Now that I narrowed it down to a story, I needed the specific thesis. I read interpretations until 3:00 a.m. when I realized that I had better get some sleep. I had to get up at 6:00 a.m., only giving me 3 hours sleep. I was really "burning the candle at both ends." I went to bed with the gloomy house of Usher on my mind and how the gloom penetrated both the characters' souls and mine. Before I fell asleep I thought about Charlie and how I never have any time for him or the kids. I fell asleep blaming myself for being a bad Mother.

Waking up the next morning was difficult. I was tired and grouchy. Charlie informed me that I am never around and need to know that construction is going to start on the house. Two men will bring the siding and windows next week. I hoped this wouldn't interfere too much with my job and with school.

The weekend came and I vowed to spend much time with Edgar Allan Poe. I slowly re-read "The Fall of the House of Usher." "With this reading, I must come up with a thesis," she thought. David stated he would go around the room and hear everyone's thesis to OK them during class. And class is almost here. I finally chose "Edgar Alan Poe's use of fear in the 'The Fall of the House of Usher' to create a Gothic atmosphere." I was not happy with this but I had to come up with something. I would find out if this was good or not.

I had a dull headache much of the time from sleep deprivation and too much caffeine. But I had to keep going. The construction was going to start on the windows. Charlie was unhappy about me not being home and staying up late several nights a week. He kept telling me that I was burning the candle at both ends. I was concerned about Literature class. My newly opened mind caused me to fight even harder to improve my current thinking and my current life. There were much higher things to think about now. And I was stuck in a rut. Mopping the kitchen floor didn't do it for me. And I was tired. I never realized that a lack of sleep combined with stress could play havoc on my body.

Completion of Research Paper

I needed to complete the Research Paper once and for all. Now that I had a thesis I could make the outline and then write. I was confident of my writing abilities.

I dedicated the evening to finishing the paper. My mood gloomily matched the topic and writing went well. Typing the paper took me well into the night.

Finally, it was finished. It was finished with my blood, sweat, and tears. And more. But it was finished. I will submit it tomorrow.

I went to bed with a dull headache and eyes wide open.

The Rain

While at work, Cindy told me to go home. She said my behavior was getting bizarre. Weird things seemed to be happening in the bookstore. The radio station was playing messages for me to pick up. I thought that I was able to read Kevin's thoughts and some of his thoughts were so funny I couldn't help but laugh out loud to myself. I wish I could get rid of the ringing in my ears.

A light rain was in the air and it further dampened my spirits. Back home, I was happy that Charles and Rose were happy to play video games upstairs. At least I didn't have to deal with them right now. I sat down with a cup of coffee. I still didn't have the urge to eat anything. I stopped being hungry days ago. Coffee was keeping me alive. And Awake. I no longer needed to sleep much at all. If I tried to sleep I would just lie there awake. The ever-changing thoughts so quickly running through my head kept me awake.

I picked up the newspaper and tried to read. I was unable to concentrate on the words. Every article seemingly presented information especially for me. Some articles were funny and I laughed out loud. Certain words stuck out as having special meaning.

The mirrors! They had to go. I wasn't allowed to see my image in a mirror. That's what the ringing in my ears told me. If I comply I will get a surprise when I do see myself. I proceeded to take down every mirror in the house. Mirrors that were too big to take down I covered with blankets. The kids asked me what I was doing. I told them "Never mind. Mom needs to do this." They looked at me funny. As I covered Rose's mirror the ring in my ears confirmed that this was the right thing to do.

After getting rid of the mirrors I turned on the radio for further instructions. A haunting song played:

> I am so in love with you
> I just can't deny it
> Everybody knows I can't deny it
> Everybody knows
> You can read me like a book
> Just like a fortune teller
> Everybody needs a fortune teller
> Everybody knows

I was immediately attracted to this song and stayed glued to the radio hoping to hear it again soon. I later learned the song was by Peter Cetera. Radio commercials provided inside information for me. I sat right on the floor by the tuner. The sound of the rain on the roof became louder.

Our dog, Calvin came over to see me. I pet him and looked into his eyes. His eyes bored into me like projectors. Jesus, help me, I'm being filmed by the cameras in Calvin's eyes. Help me to follow the instructions, Jesus. I wasn't always sure I had the instructions right—thoughts flew through my head so fast. I wanted to grab a single thought but the speed of the thoughts made it hard to focus on any one thing. I thought of the tarn-depression penetrating my soul-the kids-Charlie. I was so glad he was gone. No more put downs or being told how stupid I was. He is gone. Who cares to where. Just he is gone. That song is on again. I listened closely.

I had lots of energy. Especially now that I could do anything that I felt like doing. I was losing my inhibitions. I'm a free bird. A free spirit. I listened to the radio a while longer, trying to pick out what messages I was supposed to hear.

In a flash, Charlie burst through the back door. "What are you doing here?" I asked with horror and disgust. "I thought you were gone." "Just what is going on, here?" Charlie replied. I turned my back to him and said "I don't want you here." Charlie went upstairs. He stayed there quite a while. He disturbed me from listening to the messages on the radio.

The rain became a downpour. I saw a single flash of lightning followed by a thunderous peal. I looked out the window at the storm. I got a glimpse of myself in the window and quickly backed away. "Please help me, Jesus." I remembered that I wasn't allowed to see my reflection.

Charlie came down the steps. "Go away, I don't want you here." I ran outside into the storm. I knelt on one of the three concrete steps leading down from the street to the front yard. "Help me Jesus. Our Father who art in heaven…" the rain was cold and steady. My hair became soaked and my makeup ran. My clothes were wet and became plastered to my body. I was freezing. The lightning flashed. The thunder sounded. The neighbors started coming outside.

Charlie came outside. He grabbed me roughly by the arm and told me to go with him. Both his voice and the thunder scared me. "I don't love you anymore. I want a divorce. There's someone else." My thoughts continued racing. Kill the one you love—the tarn—the inventory—the kids—Kill the one you love…I no longer felt the freezing cold or heard the thunder.. I gave Charlie one hard push down the steps. He landed on his backside on the sidewalk. I ran back into the house to the radio waiting for me. I changed my wet clothes.

A time later a knock came on the door. I answered it. Two policemen stood there. "Are you Candace Taylor?" one of them asked. "Yes I answered cautiously. "We have a warrant for your arrest." "What?" I answered incredulously. I slammed the door in their faces.

The kids came downstairs. "What's going on, Mom?" They stood to the side not knowing where to go or what to do.

Charlie opened the door and in his company were the two policemen. One officer said, "Either you go with him or you go with us." "I'm not going with him, that's for sure." "Then you're going with us."

The police put me into the back of the cruiser. There was a cage between the front seat and the back seat. I sat quietly not knowing what was happening to me. The car pulled up to the county psychiatric hospital. They opened the door for me to get out and I bolted. I ran out into the rain, running faster and faster away from the police and the cruiser and the hospital. I zigzagged so no one could catch me. Two extra men seemingly came out of nowhere to join the chase. These two headed me off the front while the police guarded the rear. The four men caught me. All four carried me, kicking and screaming up the flight of stairs to the hospital. They carried me into an elevator. I screamed some more. They roughly put me down on a bed and started strapping down my arms and legs to the bed frame, one by one. The shadows forming on the ceiling from the lightning were so real—some appeared to be friends and some appeared to be monsters. I screamed at the top of my voice. The only sounds in the hospital room were peals of thunder and my screams--until I could scream no more.

First Day in Behavioral Health

I opened my eyes. I had no idea what time it was but I noticed some light coming through the curtains. It must be morning. Why am I left here? I felt my hands and feet tied to a strange bed in a strange room. The strap on my left hand cut into my wrist if I tried to move it. I listened carefully and heard voices outside the door. I couldn't make out what they were saying. They can't just leave me here. I am a human being. No living creature deserves to be tied to a bed and just left there. Do I hear voices? "David!" I called out. "I hear your voice!"

I heard footsteps approaching. My mouth felt so dry. I was cold. A man approached my bed. He said, "You're awake. How are you feeling now? You had quite a day yesterday." The man's voice sounded kind and concerned. "What am I doing here?" I answered. "You are in Lincoln Hospital in the Behavioral Health Unit. It provides help to people who have difficulty thinking clearly. Your bizarre behavior demonstrated some confusion. You are here so we can help you. My name is Jon. I am the Unit Coordinator. At the present time do you have any thoughts of wanting to hurt yourself in any way?" "No." I answered. "Several months ago I did but not now." "Do you have any thoughts of wanting to hurt anyone else?" Jon asked. "No." "Will you tell a staff member right away if any of these hurtful thoughts return?" "Good!" Jon replied. You can contract for safety."

Jon loosened the strap that was cutting my wrist. "If I release you, will you stay calm?" "Yes. I answered". "I am not a violent person. I don't like violence." One at a time, Jon methodically released the leather straps. First one leg, then one hand, another leg, another hand. I massaged my wrist. Jon said nothing about the wrist but looked concerned. I slowly sat up on the edge of the bed. It felt good to be able to move around again. My head was fuzzy. Nothing was as it seemed. The first thing I thought about was my kids. "Where are my kids?" "They are safe. Don't worry now. You have to take care of yourself." "I don't want to be here." I was too tired and weak to argue with anyone at the time.

Jon started saying, "Staff will be in shortly to take your vital signs and to do a strip search. Then we will see about getting you some breakfast." I wondered what the strip search was all about. Marissa RN came right away, introduced herself and asked me how I was feeling. I told her my head hurt and my wrist had an abrasion from the restraint. She said she would get orders from the doctor and he would order something for pain. She then took my vital signs and said they were stable.

Two females entered the room. One introduced herself as Paula. She told Rachel, another woman, that she was ready to start the strip search. The two women led me into the bathroom and told me to undress completely. Rachel said I have to be checked for cuts, bruises, scars, and the like. It was humiliating. I stood there completely naked while the two women looked me over and the nurse wrote on a paper periodically. "OK. You can put your clothes back on. Thank you for your cooperation." They seemed to have no compassion. They were just so cold-hearted.

Paula began to show me around the "unit" as she called it, showed me my room, and then led me to a large room with several tables and chairs. This is our "Dayroom." She introduced me to a man and to a woman who were already there. "This is John and Melanie. They too are here for help. Try to get acquainted." "But I don't need or want any help," I answered. "I have to go to work and I need to take my final exams." "After breakfast, you will meet with the doctor. You can tell him your concerns." Paula replied.

I didn't feel like talking to anyone. In the first place they were "strange" looking. "John" was elderly and just sat with his head down and didn't even look up. "Melanie" was appeared to be 30-something, blonde with black roots, was disheveled and stared at me as though I were invading her turf. I took a seat at an empty table. I didn't want to talk to either one of them. Or anyone else, I might add.

At least 10 more people came into the room at once. My table filled up with more "bizarre" people. It just then occurred to me what I must look like. I didn't have any clean clothes or makeup. I needed my curling iron. Who should I tell? I must be really strange myself.

Breakfast arrived. I had to admit that it looked pretty good. I didn't remember the last time I ate. I inhaled coffee that wasn't hot enough. My tray also offered scrambled eggs, corn flakes, milk, orange juice and a pastry. I couldn't eat it all. It was just too much. I wasn't used to eating like that.

I sat in the dayroom and watched the morning news. I worried about my job and final exams. I feared if I made any problems "they" might put me in restraints again. I needed to make a few phone calls. My head still hurt but I felt a little better after eating.

I looked out the sealed window and noticed small spiders and webs in the deep outside sills. I found them fascinating. They crawled around and they interacted with each other. They must have been there to bring me a message. They must be symbolic of something. Which spider symbolized me? I needed to study them to figure it out...

Staff came and told me the psychiatrist would see me now. I was escorted into an empty room with a desk. I saw a short, bald man about 60 years old sitting at a desk. He did not look up or even acknowledge me until the staff member left the room and shut the door.

The doctor finally spoke—"What is your name?" "Candace Taylor," I answered. "Do you know where you are?" "Lincoln Hospital." Do you know the month, day and year? I answered and got everything correct but the date was a little off. "Do you have any suicidal or homicidal thoughts?" "No," I answered. He looked up. Tell me what happened yesterday. I went on to tell him how my husband is a good man but always puts me down, yells at me and calls me stupid. I told him about Literature class and about how much David helped me to think deeply. I told him I was careful to cover up the mirrors and thought Charlie was gone but he only came back. I told him about the messages on the radio and that I needed to pray.

The doctor picked up the phone and told someone. "Come get her." I was left speechless. Paula came and escorted me out.

Back in the dayroom lunch was served. "Lunch?" You mean we have to eat again? We just ate." I tried to eat a little but had no appetite. My tray went back practically untouched. Someone told me the staff kept track of how much we ate and reported it to the nurses who wrote it in our charts. I didn't care. I didn't think that doctor was very nice to me. I asked Paula what his name was. "Doctor Hanson," she said.

I looked around at the other patients. One looked stoned and several others looked heavily sedated. Some were falling asleep in their chairs. After lunch a nurse came with a pill for me. She said it would help me relax. I innocently took the pill and went back to examining the spiders for an undetermined period of time. I felt drowsy and went to my room to lie down.

The next thing I knew, Paula was waking me up. Your caseworker, Josh is ready to see you. I quickly went to the bathroom and splashed some water on my face, being careful not to look in the mirror.

Josh greeted me as I walked in. "Hello, Candace." "I'm Josh. Please sit down." He struck me as the second most normal person in the unit, next to Jon. "It's nice to meet somebody normal here," I said. "Normal is a subjective word, Candace. It can mean anything. What's going on with you?"

"I just recently noticed that everything affects me and everything is symbolic. Plus I want a divorce."

"Wow," said Josh. "That's a lot going on. The first thing you need to do is to take all your meds. You won't get better until you do. Also, would you like your kids to come visit you?" "Yes!" I also needed to let my employer and my school know that I was in the hospital. I needed my job and an 'I' for a grade. I need to hand in my Research Paper. "Someone will do those things for you," Josh said.

I returned to my room. A short time later and much to my pleasure and surprise, Charles and Rose were brought in. "Charles, Rose," I called. I gave them big hugs and told them how much I loved them. "How did you get sick, Mommy?" Rose asked. "I don't know that I am, Honey. I don't know why I have to stay here." "Dad said you're mad at him and that's why you can't come home." I wondered if my kids were being brainwashed by their Dad.

"We brought you a whole suitcase full of clothes and here is a roll of quarters for the pay phone so you can call us." Paula brought my dinner tray to my room. I was so excited by my visitors I didn't want to eat at all. I told my kids that. Charles and Rose took the lid off the tray and began eating things. The tray was 75% eaten when the lid went back on. "Thanks." We all laughed and it felt good. I never questioned how my kids came and went. I guessed it was "magic."

After Charles and Rose left it was time for "Nurses Group Therapy." The nurse in charge said her name was Marissa. The way she talked and the way she seemed to care about the patients was a welcome change from the way the other staff seemed to act. Marissa dimmed the lights, turned off the TV and hushed everyone. "I want all of you to listen to and tell me your feelings after hearing this piece by Beethoven. It is called 'Moonlight Sonata'."

I quietly listened. I forgot how much I loved classical music. Anytime I played it Charlie shut it off because he didn't like it. He only liked rock.

Halfway through the piece tears streamed down my face. I thought about all I had lost and about how I had planned to go to college but fell in love instead. My kids. How I wanted to be a nurse, but not like those nurses. They were so cold. I am nobody.

I amounted to being a mental patient. Am I crazy? I don't want to take Basket Weaving 101 in group therapy. This music is going right through me. I am probably going to fail my classes because I can't take my final exams. Literature changed me forever. I miss David's smooth way of talking and the things he talked about. David taught me to think on a higher level. David doesn't even care about me. I do think about him though. My ears are ringing. Does he even know I'm here? Or care? I have nowhere else to go anyway. Charlie is in our house. I can't go there. I want him to go. He won't go. I settled. Some future nurse I am! I'm locked up in a mental hospital. I want a divorce. It's hopeless. I feel so helpless.

My tears turned to sobs. I wasted my life. I felt love, anger, despair, and futility. The music felt as though it was going through my very soul and pulling out mixed emotions

When the music was over and lights came on I went right to my bed. I crawled in and started shaking. A nurse came to give me some pills. I thought about what Josh said and I took the pills. I cried myself to sleep alone, resentful, and sad. I wonder if the nurses charted that.

Behavior Health Continues

I didn't sleep very well. I woke up several times in a cold sweat. The mattress was uncomfortable and the pillows were too flat. "They" took my watch so I didn't even know what time it was. Whatever was in those pills I took made me move slowly, think slowly and feel as though my brain were too heavy for my head. I just couldn't think straight.

Someone yelled into my room, "Rise and Shine." What a choice of words. Right out of "The Glass Menagerie." I finally stood up resolving not to take any more of their pills. I planned on taking them and then spitting them into the toilet and flushing them. After breakfast I did just that. To my horror one pill wouldn't flush but lay in the bottom of the toilet after several flushing. I reached into the water, picked up the pill, and embedded it into a cotton ball in my dresser. "I will fix them," I thought. "Cotton balls can be used for more than removing eye makeup."

My kids would be coming to visit again. The thought of them coming gave me something to look forward to. I appreciated them more than I ever did. Life always got in the way of true enjoyment of them. In the past I allowed lunches, homework and the rest of the routine to get in my way of appreciating them for what they were. They were, in essence, little adults, little human beings with their own thoughts, needs, and creativity. It's too bad I needed to end up in a psychiatric hospital to realize these things.

When my kids arrived Rose gave me a big hug. Of course, Charles, who was thirteen years old thought that was sissified. He made a face and we all laughed about it. We went to my room. Rose had some news for me. She told me that Dad saw the psychiatrist. Evidently, Charlie was scheduled to be evaluated too. It was unit policy to evaluate both troubled people making up the couple. I repeatedly told the staff that my husband had an anger management problem. He got nasty and snapped out when things went wrong. He often took his frustration out on either me or Charles. He yelled at us, called us names and of course, called us stupid. Rose said that Dad was bragging about the visit. According to what Charlie bragged, he offered the doctor $500.00 to say there was nothing wrong with him, that the problem was all mine. I wish I were a fly on the wall in that office. My request for help in the unit went unheeded. No wonder. Charlie paid off the Doctor. I had so hoped that we would all benefit from family counseling and possibly worked out our problems. But not now. I would have to deal alone. My heart sank. Charlie came out smelling like a rose as always.

I still wasn't thinking clearly. Although the heavy medicine wore off, I kept getting a ringing in my ears and confusion in my thinking. I didn't know what to do. I wanted a divorce. I knew that I couldn't go home.

After dinner, Kayla came to visit. I was so happy to see her. An adult who cared about me came to see me. She brought me a banana and a religious booklet about getting your life into order. I confided in her that I wanted a divorce. Kayla very matter-of- fact told me if that happens she will be on her brother's side. That was a cruel blow. I was astounded. I thought she was my friend. She and Charlie weren't even that close. I guess blood is thicker than water. She may as well have slapped me in the face. She left and I cried. I fully realized that I had no one. I was numb.

I started to hide the pills in cotton balls. They embedded very nicely. My thoughts continued to garble and I continued to make associations with pieces of literature. When 101 appeared on the clock, that was a reminder about English 101, and how it associated with my life. I fancied that my delusions were real, thinking other patients were classmates. Emily Dickinson's rose periodically ran through my mind. Fragments of other authors' creations popped in and out of my head. Thinking of Edgar Allan Poe's "The Raven" sent chills down my spine. As far as I knew, my research paper was still sitting on the desk at home. Now the paper was very late. If David refused it, I would get an F. I just wanted to know if the paper was good or not. I worked so hard on it. I endured many sleepless nights to finish the paper. I have to face David as a crazy psyche patient who couldn't handle English class. I had to face my coworkers as a Crazy who couldn't deal with my disappointment with the Inventory project. I had to deal with Charlie. It is easier to be in a psychiatric hospital. But, no, I can't give up. Charles and Rose need me. And I need them. I don't know how to get better. I feel like every path I try is the wrong one.

A short time later I was called in to see the doctor. I dreaded him. I hated him even more than ever since he accepted my husband's bribe. Maybe I should ask him what he did with the $500.00. To my surprise, a different doctor was in the room. He was dark skinned, and of far eastern decent. He spoke with an accent but was understandable. He greeted me and said, "Candace, your lithium level is 0. You can't be taking your medications. Let me explain some things to you." He spoke kindly and with great concern, something I didn't observe too much of on the unit. "I am prescribing for you 600 mg of Lithium in the morning and 600 mg at bedtime. In addition I am prescribing Abilify 5 mg in the morning. The lithium keeps your mood even. You previously exhibited periods of depression and periods of euphoria. The Abilify controls racing thoughts and will help you to think more clearly. You now need medication to live a normal life. The chemicals in your brain are not functioning properly and the medicine will regulate those chemicals. Your diagnosis is "Bipolar with Psychotic Features." I cannot emphasize how much you need this medication. I will work with you and if you get slow or groggy I will adjust the medication."

"There is one more thing, I said, "I want to divorce my husband." "Remember where you are," the doctor replied.

Several more days passed and I actually started to feel more like myself. I tried to talk to some of the other patients. I participated in group therapy. I watched TV and tried to read. I found myself less preoccupied with literature. I asked my kids to bring my textbooks so I could study a little and begin preparing for final exams.

One day I noticed a beautiful basket of flowers on a table in the dayroom. There was no card. I asked who the flowers were for. "We don't know where they came from. There was no card." The flowers contained 3 red roses with mixed flowers and lots of greens. I thought about the flowers at length. Could they be for me? Could they be from David? He must know I just disappeared from the school and from work. I hope he at least missed my presence. The red roses could symbolize the Father, Son, and Holy Spirit. Or faith, hope, and love. Or 3 poems.

Speaking of David, I have to face him to take my final exam. I have to get out of here. Maybe my caseworker could help me with my problems.

Marissa was my nurse for the evening. There was something about her that I liked. She was middle aged, plain looking, and matter-of-fact. She seemed sincere. I decided to confide in her because I had no one else. It's been so long since anyone actually listened to me. I told her I worked full time, went to school, wanted to be a nurse, and wanted to divorce my husband. She asked how old the children are. I told her they were 10 and 13. She stated that I may have more to deal with than I know. At age 13, a child may choose who they want to live with. You may not have custody of your son. Again my heart sank. I didn't know that. I didn't plan on that. Charles may very well choose his father even though Charlie isn't always nice to him. I would lose my son if I persisted. I remembered the doctor's words, "Remember where you are." I realized I couldn't divorce Charlie from a psychiatric hospital. I possibly might lose Rose too. Charlie was home working and taking care of the house and the kids. I was locked up in a psychiatric hospital. I had no support system either. I decided it was time to have a family meeting. My caseworker could set things up.

The day of the meeting I fixed my hair and makeup. I needed to look good. Charlie, Charles, and Rose were already in the room when I arrived. It was the first time I saw Charlie since my first day in the hospital. He looked thin and had dark circles under his eyes. He smiled when he saw me. I smiled back. I decided then I was going home. Maybe things will be better now. Maybe somewhere, sometime there would be happiness. We would both have to work on our relationship. I don't seem to have any other choice. It appeared that we both learned lessons. I was going home.

Going Home

My humble house looked good to me. Even the worn fence and beat-up chairs on the porch looked inviting. I was glad to return to my own familiar house. It was what it was but never did it look so good.

When we entered the house the first thing I noticed was how clean it was. Charlie must have cleaned for days. I looked at the worn kitchen table and remembered how not that long ago, I contemplated suicide. Now, however, in the middle of the kitchen table was a bud vase with a single red rose. I looked at Charlie; that was the first red rose he ever gave to me. Charlie looked at me. "Yes, that's for you," he said. "I hope you're going to take it easy for a while. You don't have to rush back to work. Use your sick time." I quickly replied, "I have many things to catch up on. I need to take my final exams so I can register for next semester. My sick time must be almost gone by now." Charlie's face dropped and he looked annoyed for an instant. He quickly recovered from his annoyance. We both left the subject drop for now. "I'll carry your suitcase upstairs for you," he said with a smile. I could tell Charlie was really trying.

I sat at the kitchen table and again thought about the suicide note. I learned so much about myself since then. I realize now I didn't really want to die, I just didn't know how to handle the rut I felt I was in. With all that happened to me the last several months, I definitely grew. And I grew up some too. I thought about what I wanted vs what I needed to do. Here I am back in my house with my family and I still need more. I will take it easy today then call

David to complete my final exam. I also need to call the school about taking my other final exams. My job is being held at The Bookstore for 30 days. I still had some sick time left, so I could afford a few days of rest. Maybe Charlie was right. Maybe I could take some more time to rest and get myself together. It was sweet of Charlie to clean the whole house and buy me a red rose. It seems he did some thinking also. Maybe the two of us could start over.

I went upstairs and took a nap in my own bed with my own pillows. It felt great and the linens smelled so fresh. I "need" to be thankful for the little pleasures in life. I shuddered thinking about the awful mattress and flat pillow in the psych unit.

I must have slept for a while. When I woke up, the house was quiet. Where were the kids? I knew in my heart that Charlie had things under control. I stretched, yawned, and went downstairs. Charlie was in the living room watching TV. He greeted me and asked if I was hungry. He had prepared some pasta with spaghetti sauce, salad, and garlic bread. We sat together at the kitchen table and ate. "Not bad," I told Charlie. He replied, "I had to learn to feed myself and the kids when you were at school." I was thrilled Charlie had accepted school that way. I realize now that I "need" Charlie and I "need" school. My "needs" seem valid to me. I can't feel satisfied with this shabby house forever. I wanted so much to be a nurse-- A respected professional with a profession within my reach. And it won't take forever to accomplish--only a few short years. I desperately want to do this.

Charlie became very serious and started telling me how he felt during my hospitalization. "I missed you more than I thought I could. You wouldn't see me. You wanted a divorce. Out of the blue I would burst into tears. I felt so helpless. I tried my hardest to take care of the kids and the house. I was the one who made sure that Charles and Rose were clean and properly dressed when I brought them to the hospital. I waited in the car when they visited. The song came on the radio about a 'Good Woman,' I sat and cried. I listened to the words and tried to make sense out of what they meant to you.

I want to play "Always on My Mind" by Willie Nelson for you. Its how I still feel about you." I was touched by Charlie's revelations. Never before would he discuss his feelings.

It was 9 p.m. and Charlie asked me if I would like to go up to bed. We walked up the steps together. I took a shower before getting into bed. Charlie took one a little earlier. We lay in bed together, Charlie's one arm around me. We lay still with no TV on tonight. We didn't make love either. It was too soon in our "new" relationship for that. I closed my eyes and tried to think forward, leaving past hurts and bad experiences behind.

The Final Exam

The next day I called the school and made arrangements to take my final exam. They would be waiting for me in the Student Support Area. Other than English, I was told I must contact my instructor. David. I will have to call or go see him. I decided to see him. I might be less awkward since I didn't consider myself a great phone person. According to the syllabus the final exam was on "The Glass Menagerie." I pretty much knew the work for all my classes. I found myself to be pretty smart in spite of being called "stupid" by Charlie for years. But I wanted to put all that behind me. All I need to do is to spend a few hours reviewing material and I should be ready for my exams.

Charlie again cooked dinner. Charles and Rose were home to eat with us. Charlie made hamburgers and macaroni and cheese out of a box. It tasted good. The four of us played "Monopoly" after dinner. I could get used to doing such things as a family.

A few days later, after reviewing, I took my final exams. Next I needed to face David. I had to get it over with. I needed to finish my English class.

David was in his office. He looked up at me with a little surprise. "Hello, Candace. It's good to see you. Are you OK?" "Yes. Thank you for asking." You don't need to be formal, Candace. It's me. Relax." David said. We both smiled. "I still need to take my final exam." David asked me if I wanted to take the final exam now. "Yes," I answered. David went to his filing cabinet and removed the test papers. I expected to go back to Student Support. Instead David said, "I have class now. You can take the test here in my office. It will be quiet and you can concentrate. I'll come back after class to see how you are doing. Good Luck!"

I thought the test was relatively easy. It was all essay questions which I generally did well on. I finished the test and left it on David's desk. I continued to wonder about the comments on my research paper. I guess I would never know. All that work and stress and I will never know. I wished I hadn't put so much stress into it in the first place. It helped cause my breakdown. In a sea of research papers, mine probably wasn't that extraordinary. It was too important to me. Looking back, I understood that now. Now if only I remember that lesson in other classes. At least I am a little wiser for the wear and tear. And wiser for having had a manic breakdown too.

On my drive home, I wondered if I would ever see David again. No doubt I would run into him on campus. He would probably continue to shop in the Bookstore. I would just have to wait and see. Some things have a way of working out. Or not working out. Some things are best left to fate.

As far as the Bookstore went, I planned on just showing up for work. I didn't want to call Angel. I wondered what kind of reception I would get from her. I decided to rest a few days before going back to work. I needed the strength to function full force. I was taking my medications faithfully. I needed to stay well. I needed to stay pulled together. I needed to take better care of myself and to reduce stress. Amen.

The Haircut

It was time for a change. I needed a new chic image. I booked a hair appointment for this afternoon. I needed a good cut because I wore my hair long and was not getting regular cuts. Often, I just slicked it back into a ponytail. I wanted a more grown-up look. I felt as though I was starting over and needed a new me. I felt a makeover would reflect my changed persona and would boost my self-confidence. I wanted to feel more chic, more sophisticated and more attractive. I wanted highlights to mix in with my blond hair. I cut out a hair picture from a magazine to take to the salon. It seemed perfect. It was chin length, flipped out at the sides and had fluffy side-swept bangs.

I arrived at the beauty salon armed with my magazine picture, good spirits, and readiness for a change. I hadn't had a haircut in so long. I chose the stylist downtown because it was close and I figured they must be pretty much the same. Her name was Charlotte. She was very nice. I enjoyed someone shampooing my hair and massaging my scalp. I then sat while an operator put foils in my hair to obtain the highlights.

Soon it was my turn in the cutting chair. Charlotte took the magazine picture and stood it up on the nearby shelf. She turned my chair away from the mirror. She sectioned off my hair and started cutting. It seemed to me that she cut and cut and cut. I observed lots of hair on the floor. Charlotte kept chatting about the downtown renovation and of how she planned on moving her salon to there. She styled my hair with a blow dryer and round brush. I couldn't feel hair around the sides of my head and the remainder of my head felt bare. She finished the style and turned my chair around to face the mirror. I looked. My hair was short. Really short. Plus it didn't look like the picture. The top was flat and lay close to my forehead. I was shocked. I immediately lifted the top with my fingers to fluff it up. I never wore my top like that. "You don't like it?" "I am just not used to it," I said. "I'm sure I'll get used to it." I paid the overpriced fee for what I got. I couldn't bear to look at my hair. It was ugly. It was unbecoming. And not at all what I wanted. I couldn't even look at myself for that matter.

I went home for a shower and re-washed my hair. I tried to work with my hair to hopefully make it look a little better. I dried my hair and tried to put in my hot rollers. My hair was so short that it barely went around the smallest roller. When I finished, it did look a little better in spite of the left side being a little longer than the right side. I felt terrible. Some makeover that was. I felt ugly. My long blonde hair was butchered.

I tried to rationalize. It's only hair. It will grow. It's not an arm or a leg. It will grow longer. In the meantime I had to live with it. It did not make me feel more attractive or self-confident. My plan backfired. Three hours and $60.00 later I wanted to stick my head in a hole like an ostrich.

I heard Charlie come home. I went downstairs to show him my hair and tell him what happened. He just said, "Not bad" and he smiled.

Life After Mental Health

I decided to go back to work next Monday. I didn't have much sick time left. Also, I needed to register for next semester. I will do that before I return to work. Charlie warned me several times not to burn the candle at both ends again. I could break down again. I knew that. And I didn't appreciate being always told about it. I need to fulfill my goal. I am going to be a nurse. The time will come when I don't have to go to school any more. Things will settle down then. For now things will remain busy. I am encouraged to continue my pursuit because I am finding out I really am smart—my grades were excellent. I couldn't dwell on my grades with Charlie. He still wants to consider me stupid. I proved him wrong.

Monday arrived. I went back to The Bookstore. I cautiously walked into the store. Cindy was there and greeted me with a big hug and a greeting to match. Even Kevin chimed in, "It's good to have you back!" Both said in unison, "I like your hair!" Let's get some celebration coffee.

Angel too said she liked my hair. She was quite nice to me and didn't bother me at all as I resumed my duties. It felt good to be back at work. I appreciated my freedom from being in a locked psych unit. I hated my hair.

I went home to a message on the answering machine "This message is for Candace Taylor. Please call Lincoln County Community College concerning your eligibility for Nursing 101. I was thrilled! I had hoped this was good news and hope I was accepted into one of the best programs in the state. I want this so very much. Acceptance to Nursing School will be the "Beginning of the End" of my goal to become a nurse.

I called and found out the news was indeed very good. I was chosen for Nursing 101 in the fall semester. A written letter would follow. I was elated! And I was hopeful. This was my big chance. I will take it! Thank you, Lincoln County Community College!

Outpatient Therapy

The next two semesters flew by. I concentrated on my grades and tried to keep track of my family. Charles and Rose were growing like weeds and Charlie seemed to be tolerant of my schoolwork. David was a memory from the past. I never saw him in the Bookstore. I guess I was a passing thing, that bright shiny new object that became dull and lackluster. I imagine he replaced me with something better. I was still grateful he came into my life even if it was for only a very short time. I guess things worked out for the best.

I felt my life was now normalized and stabilized. I was very careful to take my medications and to keep my monthly appointments. The psychiatric hospital in which I stayed ran an outpatient unit and I went there every month to get a new prescription and to talk to my Psychiatric Nurse. Joan was a little bit of a thing, about 4' 10" tall. She was somewhere in her 50's with short gray hair and with piercing blue eyes. Plain looking—no one would pick her out in a crowd, I considered her "small but mighty." When she spoke people listened. Her presence was never overlooked. She was very nice to me and I could talk freely to her about anything. I felt her empathy. Everyone should have a Joan. During my last visit Joan informed that I was doing so well that she was submitting my name to become a patient representative to Administration. I was honored to be getting some input into what goes on in the inpatient unit. Meetings were the first Tuesday of each month at 5:00. I could go there right after work.

At home, Charles and Rose were getting good grades and seemed to be well adjusted. They had lots of friends and Charles was planning for his first dance. I did the best I could to keep up with them and still take care of myself. After all, I can't take care of them unless I'm in good connection with myself. I don't want to end up in the psych unit again.

The first Tuesday of the month arrived. I arrived a few minutes early and was greeted by an older gentleman. He had gray hair, blue eyes and must have been quite handsome in his younger years. As other former patients arrived, we formed a circle and talked about what we accomplished since discharge. The older gentleman introduced himself as Robert Donning, Board of Directors. He listened to all of our input during the meeting but kept looking at me.

A few days later a letter addressed to me came from Robert Donning. In the letter Mr. Donning said how nice it was to meet me and that he would like to take me out to dinner. He also stated when the next meeting would occur. Charlie read the letter and hit the roof. He forbid me to go to any more meetings and insisted I report Mr. Donning.

I reported Mr. Donning to Joan, my psych nurse. I explained the entire incident to her and she stated he was very inappropriate. She was sorry the whole idea turned out so badly and stated that she would report him to the proper individuals.

That was such a shame. I might have enjoyed the committee and having a say. It could have been good for my growth. However, I never again heard from Robert Donning or the committee again.

Finally a Break

The months flew by quickly and it was now summer. I finished my prerequisites and general study classes for nursing school. I was so busy with work and school and family that I didn't have time to dwell on hurt feelings or misunderstandings. Charlie was treating me better. He was more attentive. His help allowed me to focus on doing what I needed to do to get through each day.

I continued to see my therapist, Joan each month. She was a godsend. I could talk to her about anything. She was supportive, understanding and non-judgmental. I looked forward to each appointment. She truly was my advocate. We talked about David at length. I came to realize that he was like a ship passing in the night. He came into my life at a time when he served a real purpose. He filled a need for real cognitive stimulation. He made me feel special. Joan convinced me that I needed to let his memory go. I became a better person for having known him. I grew. And it was time to let go.

My job became routine. I continued to do a good job but didn't put my whole heart and soul into it. Not with Angel. It was her store, her books, and no one could take any of her ownership away. She just didn't know how to share.

The kids were doing their own thing with their friends and their own activities. Charles was now 15 years old and quite a handful. Rose was 13 and quite a young lady. Charlie kept a firm handle on them and I was grateful for that. It seemed Charlie and I understood each other a little bit better even though Charlie got weird now and then. He still yelled at me on occasion, especially when things went wrong. However, I no longer stayed to be abused. I left the house when he got nasty. I guess there is no changing him. At least the outbursts were less frequent, and that was a positive change. I still have to walk on eggshells at times.

Dr. Wayne Dyer's books helped me to define myself.. I found him to be one of the most helpful inspirations in my life. His teachings caused me to rethink my purpose in life and to become a stronger person within myself. He helped keep me together. I resolved there would be no more psych wards for me.

NUR 101

My chance at Nursing School finally arrived. I, Candace Taylor, student nurse was getting the chance to become a Registered Nurse. For me this signified the beginning of the end, with my goal of being a nurse at the end. I was very grateful for the opportunity. It took a lot of hard work and sacrifice to get here. I didn't at the time realize how much hard work and sacrifice was in store for me. I made a mental note that I must take care of myself, take my meds and keep my appointments with Joan. Keeping my appointments was so easy; she was so nice to talk to and became for me a real outlet for my emotions. I blessed Joan every day. I also vowed to keep Charlie and my family happy. I could not afford another breakdown.

When I walked into my classroom I noticed how modern it was. It had seats sloping upwards like a movie theatre. I arrived early to get a good seat and chose a seat in the front row five seats from the end. This gave me a great view of the screen but was not directly in front of it.

My Nur101 professor introduced herself as Mrs. George. She was middle aged, blonde, and sounded very nice. She explained there were three components to the course—class, lab, and clinical. The class of 40 students stayed together for classroom instruction and lab but would be divided into five clinical sections of eight students each. I would have class Monday, Lab Thursday, and Clinical Tuesday and Wednesday. A tough schedule, I thought. Charlie will not be happy.

Class completely held my attention. First we learned what was expected of us, and then we started learning nursing material. Mrs. George used Power point slides and gave us a paper copy. We learned how to give a bed bath and I volunteered to demonstrate a pseudo one on a mannequin. I felt confident and did well.

My clinical group was a jovial one and we bonded quickly out of the necessity to survive. We met at a Hospital with our assignment of working on the Medical-Surgical floor. Our duties included giving or "passing" the meds, assessing patients and helping out the nurses wherever we could. Miss Smith was our Med-Surg Clinical Instructor who was also very nice. She was stern about passing medication. Before passing a med we need to tell her the right drug, dose, client, route, and time. We needed to know the purpose of the medication and common side effects. All this had to be prepared before coming to clinical. If we didn't know our stuff we couldn't pass the med. If anyone ended up failing clinical that meant you were out of the nursing program. The stress was overwhelming. Most of us had diarrhea every Tuesday and Wednesday.

I found that patients liked me and that I had a good bedside manner. I enjoyed administering care to my patients. To start, each one of us had two patients.

I spent every extra minute studying. I explained to Charlie how critical every move was in nursing school. We had people's lives in our hands. Piled in the corner were my eight textbooks and one manual. I always had reading before going to class. In lab we learned our skills such as sterile technique, inserting foley catheters, and learned how to draw up and administer IM and SQ meds. Once we passed a skill test we were allowed to practice the skill in clinical. Clinical was great except for the stress and the diarrhea.

I found myself under pressure to perform at work, school and family. It was a big adjustment in my life. I made a schedule and tried to stick to it most of the time. It was the only way I could complete everything.

Time flew by quickly. It was almost Christmas and I had the whole shopping/preparing thing to do. Charlie was a help with this. I finished the semester with a C+. This exceeded the passing score of 75 and I was eligible to go on to NUR 102 in spring semester. Life was good.

NUR 102/Part 1

Work at Barnes and Noble had become routine for me. After the inventory incident I just didn't care. I decided that was fine because I took home a paycheck and didn't feel any stress. I learned how to deal with Angel and besides, it no longer mattered. I was now in nursing school and couldn't care less about her. I now saw my job as just a paycheck.

Charlie continued to cooperate with the housework and with looking out for Charles and Rose. He was no longer as attentive as he was after my stay at the hospital. The attentiveness wore off. Just last week he nastily called me the "height of stupidity" because I asked him a question about our circuit breaker box. I said nothing in return of the nastiness. We both seemed to be falling back into our old ways—Charlie aggressive and unfeeling, and myself weak and timid. I didn't stand up for myself; I was back in the old rut.

Charlie and I further planned a much needed remodeling of the house. Charlie was making good money in security now. This enabled us to plan on vinyl siding and other new things for the house. Instead of using a general contractor, Charlie knew someone who did quality work on the side. I was happy that I wouldn't have to be ashamed of my house any longer. I was happy for Charles and Rose too. It will be better for them too. Children too are judged by what their house looks like.

I entered Nursing 102 with confidence that I would do well. I never realized just how tough it would be. I would study Obstetrics/ Pediatrics/Medical Surgical. I had 3 different classroom instructors,

3 different clinical instructors and one test for each segment. The first segment was OB.

OB passed quickly. I witnessed a live birth which was very exciting. The only drawback was that the doctor kept getting in my line of vision. I wished I could tell him to move! I made an 84 in that test. Passing in nursing was always 75 and above. I was satisfied even though I was an A student in general studies. Nursing was different. All that mattered is that I was making it.

Pediatrics was another story. The clinical teacher was not only tough but mean also. My entire clinical group was afraid of her. She screamed at us for any little incident for which we were not sure of ourselves. She made me so nervous I couldn't even draw up medicine from a vial I was shaking so badly. A classmate tried to calm me down by holding my hands steady. I ended up wasting the medicine. I didn't think the instructor would ever get over it.

I thought the PEDS rotation would never come to an end. That's just how thing seemed—unpleasant things go on forever. Also, it wasn't just PEDS. Saws were literally coming through the walls of my house and many nights I came home to rubble and a mess. One evening after school I got a very disturbing phone call. My sister, Pat had passed away.

My Sister

The phone rang. It was Aunt Lisa. She bluntly told me that my sister passed away this morning. I went numb. I knew she was sick with lung cancer and diabetes. I spoke to her every few months on the phone but didn't see her often because she lived three hours away. We sent each other cards on birthdays and Christmas. I loved her. She had the biggest heart of anyone I ever knew. I liked her husband and her two grown kids. . I didn't expect this. The last time I talked to her she told me she asked the doctor for five years. She didn't get it.

Charlie was very kind and understanding. He told me we would make the trip to the funeral and stay overnight in a motel the night before. I packed, full of memories of my sister. Growing up, she was always nice to me. She was 10 years older than me. When I was in high school she bought me beautiful outfits since she was already working. She let me wear her high school ring before I had one. I still have her ring. Somehow I never gave it back to her. It is the only possession I have of hers to remember her by.

Charlie made the trip to the funeral very pleasant. We stopped for breakfast along the way. We checked in at the "Budget Inn." The room was small but clean and efficient. It served our purpose perfectly.

As though shot by an arrow, I said to Charlie, "Charlie, I need to send flowers. There must be places in town." In the flower store tears started streaming down my face as I thought of her. "Why didn't I send her flowers when she was alive?" Then I answered myself. "Of course, I was too busy. I have work and school and I'm busy worrying about David. Now it is too late. Why couldn't we make this trip to visit her when she was alive?"

Upon entering the funeral home we noticed a big collage of pictures that were near and dear to my sister. I immediately started crying.

I could see the casket in the adjoining room. My sister was dressed in black, her favorite color. The casket was black. She had lost weight. Other than that she looked as I last saw her and she looked peaceful. I sobbed. I wanted her. We were close in spite of the distance. Now she was gone. It was now too late to tell her I loved her.

Charlie and I sat down. Mt sister's sister-in law sat and talked to us. I learned my sister couldn't walk the last few months. She never told me. She wanted to shelter me. She evidently was much sicker than she led me to believe.

Her funeral service was held in the church and was as sad as it was beautiful. The priest referred to her non-functional legs and how good-spirited and how brave she remained. I never knew. Guilt mixed with my sorrow. Someday I may meet with her again in an afterlife. I know she is in heaven.

NUR 102/part 2

I failed the PEDS test. It was so ambiguous and so difficult that the test left my mind in a blur. I must have been compromised. The professor was nice enough to hold a class to go over the test for those who failed. We were allowed to ask questions to get a better grasp on the material before we left. I thought to myself I must be the height of stupidity for failing an important exam. I couldn't tell Charlie that I failed. In his mind I suspected that he would rejoice.

MED-SURG went much better then pediatrics. Still I only made a 75 in that test. I was barely passing. Now I needed to do well in the final. I needed to study and understand the material as much as I could. The final exam was quickly approaching.

All students received a formula to figure out how many questions they could miss in the final exam and still pass the semester. My number was 30. I could miss 30 questions in the final and still pass. If I missed 31, I failed the semester.

Charlie kept warning me that I was burning the candle at both ends again. I didn't appreciate his comments. I knew the going would be tough. However, I felt no signs of decomposing. I continued to see Joan, my psych nurse, every month. She was such a Godsend. I told her about Charlie's comments about "putting me in the hospital." She told me that must make him feel very powerful. Joan was truly my advocate. She operated in my best interest, not Charlie's. Charlie accompanied me to one appointment with Joan. Needless to say, he hated her. She took away his power. She promised me that if I ever started to decompose she would talk to the psychiatrist to temporarily increase my meds until the situation passed. She promised to intervene on my behalf to keep me stable and functioning without any hospitalizations. Joan assured me I would stay together for the final exam.

I took the final exam. It was very difficult with questions from all three segments.

We took a break after taking the final exam. During our break, the professors prepared to show the test questions on the screen with the correct answers checked. First we had to remember how we answered each question. Second, we had to keep count of how many questions we missed.

I sat with pencil and paper waiting to start counting the questions I missed. First I missed one, then 6, then 9, then 20. I was getting nervous. I could miss only 10 more and still pass. As the questions dragged on, I missed 9 more. The test was almost at its end. I remembered Lab questions were at the end and I was good in math. Please, God, let me get all the rest right. I missed another. The test ended. I shook. Did I count correctly? Did I remember how I answered the ones I dwelled over? It was too close to call. I had to wait two weeks for my grade.

As it turned out, I did pass by the skin of my teeth. Skin of my teeth or not, I did pass with a C. That's all that mattered. I passed. Thank you, God. I took a deep breath and said to myself "I did it."

The Light Switch

If things weren't already tough enough with school, Charlie periodically continued having his outbursts. I needed Joan, my Psychiatric Nurse. My monthly appointment was scheduled for today between work and school. I wondered if I could make my schedule any tighter. I had no one else in which to confide my true feelings. Charlie certainly doesn't and can't understand me. I couldn't wait to see Joan about an incident that just recently happened.

Joan greeted me in the waiting room. While walking to her office, we exchanged the usual meaningless greetings. "What's on your mind, Candace?" Joan asked. I immediately started spilling my guts.

"I walked into Rose's room and turned on the light switch. The power blew. 'What happened?' Charlie asked. 'All I did was turn on the light,' I answered. Charlie went looking for a flashlight to fix the circuit breaker. I immediately shut off the light switch. 'Come here,' Charlie ordered. I anxiously answered, 'Coming!' and ran up the steps.

'Come here,' Charlie repeated. 'This is a small flashlight. You turn it on with a rocker switch.' I noted that was the strangest looking flashlight I ever saw. I felt all sides in the dark and couldn't find the rocker panel switch. I felt Charlie's impatience growing. "It's on the front. Do you know the front from the back? How the f--- stupid are you?" He then put my finger on the rocker panel. The angrier he became the more unable to function I became. He turned on the flashlight.

My next job was to shine the light into his work area. I very carefully held the light where he was working on the light switch. I thought I was doing pretty well when he changed his position. 'I said, keep the light where I'm working, not over there.' I wanted to respond with something nasty myself, but if I did he would throw down the tools and quit fixing the light. I had to bite my tongue and continue being yelled at or face the consequences. One of his sayings was, 'I don't get even, I get ahead.' No wonder I am in therapy. I can't ever let out my frustrations without facing bad consequences."

Joan quietly listened. She said, "This is not the first story of Charlie putting you down whenever a problem arises. Things are not always your fault. He seems to have a very low boiling point. This is called "Intermittent Explosive Disorder." He loses control when things are not smooth for him. This requires therapy. Would he come in for therapy? I knew Charlie well enough to know that he would never accept therapy. Of course he doesn't have a problem, again, only I do. He would never even admit he had a problem, let alone accept help.

My time was up. I thanked Joan for listening. I felt better having talked about it. Joan was my outlet. It was confidential. It gave me insight into my problems. "Thank you, Joan," I said ever so gratefully.

NUR 203

NUR 203 proved to be even more difficult than NUR 102 was. This semester brought only two tests and a final exam. The first test was cardiac and the second psychiatric nursing.

I failed the Cardiac test. Little did I realize that because of that I would have to face the very impressive Dr. Delaney, Dean of Nursing? I was in trouble. Sixty-fours do not bring commendation. I was worried. I can't fail now. I have come too far.

I walked to Dr. Delaney's building and waited outside her office for a seemingly endless period of time. What would she say to me? Would I be or put on academic probation or dismissed from school? My insecurities grew as I waited.

Eventually, I was escorted into the Dean's office. Her office décor was decorated with mauve and burgundy walls. It was the most stylish office that I had ever seen. Dr. Delaney was seated at her desk. She was dressed in a red two piece skirt suit and wore matching red pumps. She looked stunning. She held a full size yellow pencil in her hand. The look on her face was one of concern.

She did not invite me to sit. She greeted me by bluntly saying, "Candace Taylor you are here because you scored a 64 in the cardiac test. Would you want a nurse like that taking care of your family? What happened?" Her questions and her directness floored me. I answered, "I did study for the test but found cardiac to be difficult. I thought I knew the material. I even studied with a group." I felt my knees shaking.

"Let me tell you a story," she said. "When I was in nursing school, I never failed a test. However, I came close to failing one. I remember the terror of reading each question and not knowing the answer. It sounds like you need help with your study habits."

Dr. Delaney opened the file cabinet and brought out my NET test results. "Candace, you are a 100% visual learner and a 100% written learner. You are also a solitary learner. You don't learn in a group. You need to look at words and pictures. "No one explained that to me quite like that. I didn't understand my test results. I will do better. I said to Dr. Delaney, "I will do better. I want very much to be a nurse."

I could not read Dr. Delaney's expression. She was so controlled. She continued, "You need to bring up the 64 and there is only one more test before the final exam. That means the 64 is 1/3 of your grade. To pass the course you need to finish with at least a 75. It can be done. And you can do it. Eat, sleep, and breathe nursing school if you have to. Set your priorities and keep a study schedule. I expect to get better reports on you. The Dean dismissed me and turned her back to me. I left her office both enlightened and discouraged.

Failing out of nursing school would destroy me dream. My husband would be thrilled to see me fail. Then he really would call me stupid. What an example I would set for my kids. *The mother who failed nursing school*: I would have to tell my coworkers that I failed. I have to make it. I will make it. Even Dr. Delaney said it can be done. I am not dead in the water yet. I am going to be a nurse.

NUR 203/part 2

Cardiac was over. The next segment was Psychiatric Nursing. I banked on this as being my rotation to succeed. I needed to do very well to pass. I always had that stress over my head. I was an A student! Until I hit Nursing School. Now I am always worrying about passing instead of worrying about getting an A. I needed an A in the psych test to bring up the 64 I made in the cardiac test. I made myself a vow to do this. It seemed I had everything going for me now. Psych was my segment. That is what I wanted to do as my career. I was very interested. I wanted to know everything. The Clinical Rotation was scheduled at Third Street Hospital—the only large psychiatric hospital in the area. I couldn't wait to start this rotation.

To my horror and astonishment, in walked Nurse Marissa! She took the teacher's seat in front of the class. Oh, No! She knows all about my private problems and all about my psychiatric condition. She was wonderful in the unit, but what about class? She would probably recognize me as one of her former patients!

Nurse Marissa introduced herself as Mrs. Keeney. She stated that she was an adjunct professor who worked in the field as a Psychiatric Nurse. I noticed the class responding to her just as I had in the unit. I felt more at ease as she talked. After class I was too timid to approach her to clear the air. I just left quickly without a word.

As it turned out, Marissa Keeney was my professor for class but not for clinical. My clinical instructor was Lynn Packer. I hoped for a better rotation and better experience than I had with some rotations, particularly the PEDS rotation. I was in Behavior Health! Yes! My rotation! I knew this was what I wanted to do.

The hospital itself was very impressive. Each unit was locked with heavy doors with the name of the unit posted on the door. Administration gave Mrs. Packer a set of keys which appeared to have a key for each unit. I wondered how she knew which key was which.

My experience at Third Street Hospital was a positive one. As it turned out, we weren't allowed to do very much except talk to the patients. We weren't allowed to pass meds or to chart. However, we were allowed to do group therapy in the adolescent unit. The hospital had books full of ideas to talk about. In some books we copied pages full of questions for the patients to answer. The patients received pencils with dull points to use during the questions. The pencils were counted and collected after group. Staff took every precaution so the patients did not have anything accessible to hurt themselves..

Other safety issues were apparent throughout the hospital. Patients were not allowed to have belts, shoelaces, scarves, or any sharp object on their person or within their grasp. Staff searched every bedroom at start of shift for contraband. I thought about my own hospitalization. During searches, no one ever suspected that my meds were embedded in cotton balls.

Patients took turns answering the patient phone. Patients were allowed to make and receive calls between 7:00 and 9:00 p. m.

I was impressed enough that I knew I wanted to work there after graduation. I now had a specific goal.

Back in class, Nurse Marissa treated me no differently from anyone else. I was active in class. The psychotropic medications were difficult to learn and there were a lot of them. Test day came and I scored a 92.

Nurse Marissa and I never discussed my hospitalization. She did tell me my 92 was high score of the class. She gave me a pleased smile and told me to think like this: "Candace Taylor, Psychiatric Nurse." I completed the semester with a C+.

NUR 204 - Last Semester of Nursing School

I entered my last semester of Nursing School with a positive attitude ready to take on the world. Last semester's great ending had my totally hyped up. Charlie was still not that supportive about school. Though I must say I showed him I'm not as stupid as he always called me. Rose told me that he said he had hoped that I would fail. Is that what he wants for me, the person he supposedly loves? What kind of love is that?

I still enjoyed my monthly appointments with Joan. She kept me thinking positively and was so proud of my nursing school endeavor. She did not want to jinx me; she told me to work harder than ever and not slack off now. Becoming an RN was within grasp's reach. I needed to work with my goal in mind.

Clinical for this semester was all Med-Surg. The clinical instructor, Miss Jones, was really tough on us. She was very by-the-book and demanded excellence. She checked our Nurses Notes before we could write in the chart. She was a perfectionist. Clinical meant diarrhea every Tuesday and Wednesday.

To prepare for clinical we went to the hospital for our assignments on Monday evening after Lab. That was still another late night. Then we had to make drug cards for every drug we were to give. From the cards we needed to know the drug, dose, client, route, time and correct documentation.

It was a long clinical semester. We hung IV's and gave injections. We were being prepared for the real world. Toward the end of the semester the school required us to work two consecutive 12 hour shifts. Miss Jones would have her watchful eye checking our performance. The two days passed very quickly. I had four patients and was keeping the pace. I felt my energy level was high in spite of very little sleep and much stress. I was staying together. Thank goodness for Psych meds and for Joan.

My entire clinical group passed the two day test. I was so ecstatic, as we all were. Miss Jones bought hoagies and soda for the entire floor in celebration. I realized now that she was so tough on us so that we could survive.

For some reason, the classroom final exam didn't seem as difficult as prior exams. "Was the exam easier or am I getting better?" I thought. The test review signified a final grade of 80 for me. I passed the last semester with a margin to spare. My final grade was a B. I did it! I was a Graduate Nurse! But the goal is not yet completed. I must pass State Boards. And I'll do it!

After Nursing 204

All Graduate Nurses were to be honored at a breakfast where they would be pinned by the Dean of Nursing, Dr. Delaney. Each graduate was allowed to bring their family. Even Charlie agreed to attend the breakfast. One by one the Grads were called up by name and pinned by Dr. Delaney. This signified the beginning of our Nursing careers. The State Board of Nursing allowed GNs to work for one year while they prepared to take State Boards. Dr. Delaney told all the Grads that the sooner you take State Boards the better the chances of passing. My appointment to take the exam was three months away.

I tried to maintain normalcy in my household and job while I studied for exams. With school over, my schedule allowed me to breathe and to get some sleep.

I understood each GN would take the computerized test and would get from 75 to 250 questions to answer. Each question answered correctly or incorrectly determined the difficulty of the next question.

I reviewed for the test as much as I could. When the day came, I had apprehensions. I knew from Nursing School that the first impression of the answer was usually correct.

My appointment for State Boards arrived. As I answered each question the question number 75 came up. I answered it. It did not shut off. Question 76 came up. I kept answered the questions. Question 150 came up. It did not shut off. Then 200 came. I was getting mentally and physically drained. After question 250, the concluding screen finally came up. I was exhausted. "Just my luck to get all 250 questions," I thought.

I waited the 2 days for my pass or fail grade. While holding my breath, I logged onto the computer in the bookstore for my final results. "Please, God, let me have passed. The screen came up. Candace Taylor, Registered Nurse. The tears rushed out of my eyes. I felt like 1000 pounds had been lifted from my shoulders. All I could do was cry.

I had many people to thank-- Charlie, who took care of the house and the kids, Charles, Rose for their support, Joan and my professors. I must thank Kayla, who started the whole process with financial aid. And I must thank David, whose help kept me from going under. I will not forget David. Above all, I thank God. It must have been your will for me to become Candace Taylor RN.

Graduation

My entire family accompanied me to graduation. They bought me a dozen red roses to carry. I was so excited to receive my Associate's degree in Nursing. My family went to their seats while I went to the line-up on the bottom floor. The Arena buzzed with the activity. I found a few of my classmates and we took pictures.

The faculty was dressed in their professional attire. I saw David with a few students talking animatedly. They were in a circle and seemingly having a good time. I mustered up some bravery and walked over. David saw me approach. He gave me a big smile and said, "Here it is, the pot of gold at the end of the rainbow." I smiled back. He was very nice. I just wanted to make peace with him and say goodbye. After all, I messed up, not him. David asked what my future plans were. "To get a Nursing job," I replied. We both laughed.

The group he was talking to dispersed. Before he walked away he said, "Candace, you have special way about you. Don't ever lose that."

I was grateful for those words. He gave my something to take with me.

My First Nursing Job/Orientation

Cindy and Kevin threw a little party for me at work. Even Angel ate a piece of cake and told me congratulations. I told her I would not be leaving The Bookstore just yet. First I had to stabilize my life without all the studying and stress of Nursing School.

At my last session with Joan, she told me I needed to "feel" like a professional. Just a few years earlier I was serving pizza and beer in a pizza tavern. Now I am a professional. But there is something missing. I hope feeling like a professional comes soon. I really hope it comes soon.

I applied to my beloved Third Street Hospital for a nursing job. There was a 3-11 part time opening in the Children and Adolescent's Unit. I had enjoyed that unit during clinical rotation and even did some group therapy there. It seemed like a fit. The interview went well and the Nurse Manager hired me on the spot.

Charlie and I told anyone who would listen that I got a nursing job at Third Street Hospital. Charlie was proud of me now. Think of the salary. I was so excited. This was my dream job. I couldn't wait to start.

I went through a week's work of preliminary blood and urine tests. I attended a group session presented by the HR manager. He also held a session about insurance and rules of employment. One rule stated that employees were forbidden to befriend or accept any gifts for having taken care of someone while a patient. What were the consequences for doing this? You would lose your job.

I reported for my first day of on-the-job orientation. No one could have been more thrilled than me. My dream job. Here it was. All that hard work was paying off. I would orient 2 days dayshift then 3 evenings on evening shift, the shift I would be working.

I was escorted into the Children's and Adolescents Unit by security. They led me into the unit and the huge, heavy door locked behind me. It was Saturday which seemed a bit strange to be orienting on that particular day. I entered the Nurse's Station— who was standing there but Leonard R, my ex-boyfriend from High School! That relationship ended badly. I was too immature to handle it. He stood glaring at me, all 5"8" of him. He had dark hair and a full beard. He wasn't exactly what I consider handsome but he wasn't plain either. He did not smile. We hadn't seen each other in years. However, he was now standing in the Nurses' Station with me looking on. With him was another person who introduced herself as "Jean." Jean was in her late 30's with short blonde hair and kind of pretty but not exceptionally so. Her hair was a little messy. Jean said, "We've been expecting you." She and Leonard both made me feel as though I were an invader with two heads.

I was given a very brief description of the unit routine. Both children and adolescent patients get up in the morning, get their vital signs taken and go to the cafeteria for breakfast. Then they had school right in the hospital. "What a great idea," I thought. "They won't fall behind in their schoolwork." While the patients were in school, we did room searches and charted on their behavior. "This seems easy," I thought. Leonard and Jean told me to read charts until the end of the shift.

The first day of orientation was uneventful. Leonard and Jean would eat snacks together and not even invite me to join them. I felt like such an outsider. I later learned that at one time they dated, but no longer.

The second day of orientation Leonard told me to take patient vital signs manually with a cuff and stethoscope. I was a nervous wreck. It was a skill in nursing school and I remembered asking the lab teacher for extra help. I still wasn't good at it. During my hospital rotation I used the automatic Dina map machine. You just put on the cuff and the machine did the rest. Now I need to perform manually.

I fumbled. I tried. I told Leonard I couldn't hear the diastolic. He snatched the stethoscope and listened himself. "120/78. Real easy."

I wanted so desperately to fit in. This was my dream job, the conclusion to a lifetime of dreaming and a long time of studying. I compromised my family to get here. So far, things were not going well. Evening shift will be better—it had to be better than this. I would get my own keys to the unit when I started evening orientation. I smiled at that. My very own keys to Third Street Hospital.

At home I told Charlie about my experience. He didn't call me stupid. He even seemed sympathetic. He told me I really need to practice blood pressures. "You can practice on me," he said. I immediately went to get my stethoscope. Charlie had good loud sounds and I heard the beats perfectly. I thanked him and told him he helped enormously. Charlie looked pleased.

Monday evening arrived and it was time to start my first evening shift of orientation. My Nurse Manager, Debra was waiting for me. She was 50+ years old, about 5'6" tall and somewhat stout. She had short brown hair and looked professional. I was uncomfortable around her. I wasn't sure she even liked me. However, that could have been all in my imagination. I wonder what Leonard and Jean told her about me. She handed me the set of keys. I rejoiced inside. Debra told me to keep them in my car. That way I would always have them.

Debra then introduced me to Roslyn. It was the same Roslyn I graduated with just four months ago. How could that happen? Evidently she was full time and I was scheduled to work on her days off. Evidently until I was hired she got a lot of overtime.

Roslyn had not yet taken her state boards. She was very thin and wore her long dark hair in a ponytail. I remembered her from class. She was the one crying in her seat after the final exam review.

Debra and Roslyn chatted a bit about the patients then Debra left me to Roslyn. Roslyn told me there are 2 techs working under us and they pretty much know their jobs. They each charted on the 2 patients you assign them and you chart on the rest. You take the harder patients. I will introduce you to the techs. You are in charge of them. Stay with them a few hours so you learn what they do. The first tech I met was a female. She looked hard core and acted as though she owned the unit. Her name was Terry. I could tell she was a veteran worker at the hospital. She knew her job and she knew the ropes. I got the feeling that she didn't appreciate reporting to a brand new nurse. The second Tech was a male named Joe. He seemed nicer than Terry. Roslyn told me that Jim sometimes works in the unit also. He was off tonight. So this was my staff—I had no experience supervising staff. What was I supposed to do with them? Roslyn told me to learn their jobs, which right now was watching the patients. The techs left me to watch the movie with the patients.

I thought that maybe they had a lunch break or something. After "Bewitched' was over I thought we would discuss the movie. Bewitched was a poor choice for discussion. Then Terry appeared with a Sudoku book in her hand. I asked her what we do when the movie is over. She said it's free time until group. I saw several patients lined up at the phone. They were so young. Some of them needed change. Fortunately I had several quarters and could accommodate them. I made a mental note to bring a roll of quarters from home.

I liked the kids. It's too bad some of them had really big problems to deal with. I knew this from reading the charts on dayshift. This is evening shift, my shift. So far, no one had accepted me. Roslyn walked to the dayroom to see how I was doing. I told her that I needed to know what she was doing. We walked back to the Nurse's Station together and she went into a room off to the side. I followed her in and she snapped "I just threw something away." I apologized.

I was still on a high and still thrilled to be working at Third Street Hospital. "I am the nurse. I am in charge. This is my unit. Just the other day I was telling my LPN neighbor how great it was to have a job at Third Street. My Nurse Manager gave me extra orientation with Roslyn. I thought I knew the job. I was able to pass meds and chart. Roslyn told me that the techs watch the patients. I never learned the admission and discharge paperwork because, how ironically, all the admissions came on dayshift. Another drawback was the keys. I could never get them to open the locks on those great heavy doors. I knew staff was laughing at me for this. I didn't know how to correct the problem. If there was a trick, no one showed me. One time I quickly walked in with another staff member so I didn't have to use those keys myself.

Aside from loving the keys but hating how they functioned, I loved working at Third Street Hospital. I loved being the nurse. I was proud to work there. Everyone that I knew, knew that I was here. And I was so proud.

First Nursing Job Part 2

At the beginning of the next shift, Debra was waiting for me. She told me she wasn't sure of my ability to take charge of the unit. She was taking me to HR to receive some extra orientation. Debra said the hospital often hired new nursing grads from Lincoln County Community College and there was never a problem. I wondered how she even knew what kind of job I was doing. She was never present on my shift. She must have heard it from the grapevine. Evidently the grapevine didn't have much good to say about me.

Back on the unit, I noticed several new patients. The one girl was heavy and had Juvenile Diabetes. She was a whiner and had some borderline characteristics. She was needy and attention seeking. I could see why she needed to be hospitalized. Another young man and a young lady were new and they seemed very interested in each other. Evidently, teen-age hormones are just as strong in mentally disturbed teens as they are in normal teens. Several "regular" patients were still on the unit.

Unfortunately my orientation was still with Roslyn. I wished I had a more experienced person who oriented new nurses before. She is only a nurse a few months herself and never oriented anyone. I sensed that Roslyn didn't know how to orient me. Debra sensed that I am not comfortable in my own shoes. Just like Charlie, she, too, probably considered me stupid.

I took the patients to the cafeteria for dinner. They appeared to be somewhat rowdier than usual. I watched them closely. One of them was giving the cafeteria worker a hard time about a grilled cheese sandwich. Terry, my hard core tech, quickly went over and resolved the situation.

Our return to the unit gave my patients an hour free time before group time. Group was eight o'clock. . I watched the lovey-dovey couple so they didn't get too chummy. Another female teenager was watching them too. I had a hard enough time learning their names.

Group came. Roslyn did Group and I was spectator. She told the kids to sit in a circle and play "Pictionary." There was a drawing board set up for them. With every correct answer they would change seats and yell out "Taco Salad." She must have made up this variation herself. Play continued for a while but being given teenagers, it became rowdy. Play had to be discontinued and group session was over.

I was left alone with the teenagers. They had free time until meds. They were stirred up from the game. I needed to check the diabetic girl's blood sugar to see if she needed insulin coverage at bedtime. Rosalyn had showed me how to use the machine one time a few days ago. I thought I remembered what to do. This time the machine came up as "controls." I did not know what to do so I let it go a while. I didn't know who to ask for help as I was in charge of the unit. I prepared the meds for bedtime into their little cups. I came out of the med room and the couple out of my watch were making out on a table. Just then, a patient started pulling at Josh and Chris, the two potential lovebirds, to make them stop. She too had a crush on Josh and wasn't going to stand for their attentiveness. SHE wanted him. The patient with diabetes started yelling, "I want my blood sugar tested!" I tried to assure her that she would have it tested. "I want it tested now!" By this time the two girls were in a scuffle and just "WHERE WERE MY TECHS?" A supervisor came out from nowhere and called the Doctor. The Doctor was in another unit and quickly came to the Children and Adolescent Unit. In the meantime other teens started protesting that they want their meds. The unit was in chaos.

The Doctor started writing orders for seclusion in others areas of the hospital. He said each needed to go somewhere. Help came in from other units. Debra, my Nurse Manager was called. She arrived on the unit very unhappy. She ordered me to start giving my meds out. She asked why I didn't give them anti-anxiety medication when they started acting out? I honestly answered I didn't know enough to do that. All I ever gave was the medication they always get on schedule. She looked at me like I was stupid and walked away. Debra did the controls and got the machine to work. She gave the needed insulin.

By now, most of the unit was in seclusion in different areas. Our unit could not hold all the patients who needed a quiet room.

The shift ended. I walked outside and there was Debra talking to some people smoking a cigarette. "I will see you in the morning in HR," she said

I drove home wondering what my fate would be. The tears streamed down my face. Where were my techs? What is wrong with me? What the hell happened?

Charlie was sleeping. I quietly sat at the old computer and started composing my letter of resignation. Tears turned to sobs. I felt so alone, so useless. My dream job. What happened? All that school, all that studying, and all that clinical. What will I do now? It was all in vain. It was wasted. My new career was over. I am a failure. I finished the letter and quietly cried myself to sleep.

Meeting in HR

I waited outside the HR's door awaiting my own fate. I possessed the letter of resignation in my purse.

The director of HR came for me. Debra was already in his office, evidently giving the story from her perspective. She didn't waste any time. The director was very kind in manner. I told him I prepared a letter of resignation. "Where is the letter?" I reached in my purse and offered it to him. He quickly took it. I prepared the letter with a two week notice. "We don't need the two week notice," he said. "But it can go into your file with it. Do you have the keys?" I thought my heart was going to break. I again reached into my purse and handed over the keys. I was dismissed. It was officially over. Terminating my job took about 5 minutes. At the time I didn't even think how I would explain this to all the people who I told about this great new job. I just ached, and I carried emptiness within me.

Cautious New Hope

Several weeks passed. I continued working at The Bookstore because management there quickly hired me back. I knew that I had outgrown being a store clerk. But it was a paycheck. And I still loved the store.

My heartache and humiliation over my first nursing job still haunted me. But the more I thought about it, in my heart, I knew I didn't want to waste that education. I still very much wanted to be a nurse. But where could I go? I had to start over because I could never use Third Street Hospital as a reference.

Charlie came in with the newspaper in his hand. He sat at the kitchen table engrossed in it. Suddenly he said, "Candace, listen to this. One of the patients hung himself in Lincoln Memorial Behavioral Unit. Everyone was fired. More than likely, no one will know you were a patient there because they were all fired. Maybe you can get a nursing job there."

I recollected my experience as a patient in Behavioral Health. I knew I could do a better job than the previous staff. The answer seemed clear. I had to try. At this point, what did I have to lose?

Resolution

I gingerly went to the office building of Lincoln Memorial. Memories of my own hospitalization haunted me. I had to put that behind me. I even managed to stay together after the Third St Hospital incident.

I saw a sign called Human Resources. I entered the door and was greeted by a female receptionist. "How may I help you?" she asked with a smile. I would like to fill out a job application for Psychiatric Nurse. I had no resume. I was not using my few weeks at Third Street Hospital as experience because it ended so badly. This was like a shot in the dark.

I filled out their application. They required you identify any medications you used daily. I wrote lithium carbonate, abilify. I worried if this came out later and if I were hired I would lose my job over not disclosing. So I was honest concerning this right from the start.

A few days later, Charlie, Charles, Rose and I went out to dinner. Charlie and I really had to be proud of our offspring. They grew up well-adjusted in spite of a mother in school.

Our family arrived home to find a message on the answering machine addressed to Candace Taylor. Please come to Lincoln Memorial HR Office for a job interview on Tuesday at 2:00. Please ask for Mrs. Walters.

I was so grateful. No whooping or dancing this time. I matured a lot since I first found out I had received the financial aid. Third Street Hospital was my first chance. Now I am getting a second chance. It's in God's hands.

Printed in the United States
By Bookmasters